CENTER STAGE

Express Yourself in English

1

Irene Frankel

Series Consultants

MaryAnn Florez

Sharon Seymour

PEARSON
Longman

Center Stage 1: Express Yourself in English

Pearson Education, 10 Bank Street, White Plains, NY 10606

Staff credits: The people who made up the *Center Stage 1* team—representing editorial, production, design, and manufacturing—are John Barnes, Elizabeth Carlson, Tracey Cataldo, Dave Dickey, Christine Edmonds, Shelley Gazes, Laura LeDréan, Melissa Leyva, Gabriela Moya, and Robert Ruvo.

Cover art: Gilbert Mayers/SuperStock

Photo Credits: p.4 Ryan McVay/GettyImages; **p.5** (first) Kevin Peterson/AgeFotoStock; (second) Andersen Ross/AgeFotoStock; (third) Kevin Peterson/AgeFotoStock; (fourth) Amos Morgan/AgeFotoStock; **p.8** (top left) Blend Images/AgeFotoStock; (top right) Kevin Peterson/AgeFotoStock; (middle left) Royalty-Free/Corbis; (middle right) Glow Images/AgeFotoStock; (bottom left) Dana Neely/AgeFotoStock; (bottom right) Michael N. Paras/AgeFotoStock; **p.13** (top left) Peter Kramer/GettyImages, (top right) Elisabetta Villa/GettyImages; (second left) Otto Greule Jr./GettyImages; (second right) Hubert Boesl/dpa/Corbis; (third left) Frazer Harrison/GettyImages; (third right) Anthony J. Causi/Icon SMI/Corbis; (bottom left) Chung Sung-Jun/GettyImages; (bottom right) Stephane Cardinale/People Avenue/Corbis; **p.17** (top to bottom, left to right) Hill Street Studios/AgeFotoStock; SuperStock/AgeFotoStock; rubberball/AgeFotoStock; Johnny Stockshooter/AgeFotoStock; Esbin-Anderson/AgeFotoStock; Walter Bibikow/AgeFotoStock; Esbin-Anderson/AgeFotoStock; Mago World Image/AgeFotoStock; Barbara Laws/AgeFotoStock; Jose Fuste Raga/AgeFotoStock; IT Stock Free/Royalty-Free/JupiterImages; Wojtek Buss/AgeFotoStock; **p.18** (top row, left to right) BananaStock/Alamy; Digital Archive Japan/Alamy; BananaStock/Alamy; Great American Stock/IndexStock Imagery; Stockbyte Platinum/Alamy; (bottom row, left to right) MIXA Co., Ltd./Alamy; foodfolio/Alamy; foodfolio/Alamy; foodfolio/Alamy; **p.19** (clockwise from top left) BananaStock/Alamy; Burke/Triolo Productions/JupiterImages; foodfolio/Alamy; foodfolio/Alamy; **p.21** (top left) Mike Grey/GettyImages; (top right) Junko Kimura/GettyImages; (middle left) Fotos International/GettyImages; (middle right) Stephane Cardinale/People Avenue/Corbis; (bottom left) Susana Vera/Reuters/Corbis; (bottom right) Rune Hellestad/Corbis; **p.22** (top row, left to right) Royalty-Free/Corbis; foodfolio/Alamy; Cephas Picture Library/Alamy; (bottom row, left to right) BananaStock/Alamy; BananaStock/Alamy; **p.23** (top row, left to right) Royalty-Free/Corbis; Angelo Cavalli/GettyImages; Pete Saloutos/Corbis; (bottom row, left to right) Photodisc/GettyImages; Barry Lewis/Corbis; **p.25** (first) Stephane Cardinale/People Avenue/Corbis; (second) Digital Archive Japan/Alamy; (third) BananaStock/Alamy; (fourth) foodfolio/Alamy; (fifth) MIXA Co., Ltd./Alamy; (sixth) Fotos International/GettyImages; (seventh) foodfolio/Alamy; (eighth) foodfolio/Alamy; (ninth) foodfolio/Alamy; (tenth) BananaStock/Alamy; (eleventh) Susana Vera/Reuters/Corbis; (twelfth) Cephas Picture Library/Alamy; (thirteenth) Royalty-Free/Corbis; (fourteenth) Mike Grey/GettyImages; **p.29** (top left) Glow Images/AgeFotoStock; (top right) Corbis/JupiterImages; (middle left) Michael N. Paras/AgeFotoStock; (middle right) VStock LLC/AgeFotoStock; (bottom left) ImageSource/AgeFotoStock; (bottom right) Medio Images/AgeFotoStock; **p.32** Steve West/GettyImages; **p.33** (top row, left to right) Glow Images/AgeFotoStock; Blend Images/AgeFotoStock; Digital Vision/AgeFotoStock; Tim Flach/GettyImages; (bottom row, left to right) Mike Kemp/AgeFotoStock; Glow Images/AgeFotoStock; Purestock/AgeFotoStock; Lilly Dong/JupiterImages; **p.41** (top left) Sergio Pitamitz/Corbis; (top right) rubberball/AgeFotoStock; (middle left) Kevin Peterson/AgeFotoStock; (middle right) Henryk T. Kaiser/AgeFotoStock; (bottom left) BananaStock/JupiterImages; (bottom right) BananaStock/JupiterImages; (bottom) Frazer Harrison/GettyImages; **p.78** C Squared Studios/GettyImages; **p.80** Jack Hollingsworth/Brand X Pictures/JupiterImages; **p.82** (left) Mark Scott/GettyImages; (right) Gregory Costanzo/GettyImages; **p.83** (left) Mark Scott/GettyImages; (right) Gregory Costanzo/GettyImages; **p.85** (clockwise from top left) Wei Yan/Masterfile; Tony Metaxas/GettyImages; Thomas Northcut/GettyImages; Stockdisc/GettyImages; Thomas Northcut/GettyImages; Jack Hollingsworth/GettyImages; David Schmidt/Masterfile; **p.100** (top) BananaStock/Alamy; (bottom) Burke/Triolo Productions/JupiterImages; **p.116** George Doyle/Stockbyte Platinum/GettyImages; **p.126** (top left) Inmagine/Alamy; (top right) blphoto/Alamy; (middle left) image 100/Alamy; (middle right) Wally McNamee/Corbis; (bottom left) Bubbles Photolibrary/Alamy; (bottom middle) Stock Connection Distribution/Alamy; (bottom right) Imageshop/Alamy; **p.127** (top) Art Vandalay/GettyImages; (middle) PCL/Alamy, (bottom) David Stoecklein/Corbis; **p.140** Inspirestock Royalty-Free/FotoSearch; **p.153** (top row, left to right) Michael Newman/PhotoEdit; David Young-Wolff/PhotoEdit; BananaStock/AgeFotoStock; (bottom row, left to right) Royalty-Free/Corbis; Royalty-Free/Corbis; Gabe Palmer/Corbis; **p.182** (top left) Abode/Beateworks/Corbis; (top middle) Big Cheese Photo LLC/Alamy; (top right) David R. Frazier Photolibrary, Inc./Alamy; (bottom left) Royalty-Free/Corbis, (bottom right) Janine Wiedel Photolibrary/Alamy; **p.183** (top to bottom) Royalty-Free/Corbis; Brand X Pictures/Alamy; ImageState/Alamy; ImageSource/Alamy; Jutta Klee/Corbis; **p.189** Royalty-Free/Corbis

Text composition: ElectraGraphics

Text font: 12.5 Minion

Illustrations: 101/A Corazón Abierto (Marcela Gómez), Steve Attoe, Kenneth Batelman, Marty Harris, Brian Hughes, Stephen Hutchings, Robert Kemp, Luis Monteil, Francisco Morales, Chris Pavely, Precision Graphics, Mari Rodríguez, Roberto Sadí, Gerardo Soria, John Schreiner, Gary Torrisi, Chris Vallo.

Library of Congress Cataloging-in-Publication Data

Frankel, Irene.
  Center stage. — 1st ed.
    p. cm.
  Contents: 1. Beginning / Irene Frankel — 2. High beginning / Lynn Bonesteel and Samuela Eckstut — 3. Intermediate / Lynn Bonesteel and Samuela Eckstut — 4. High intermediate / Lynn Bonesteel and Samuela Eckstut.
  ISBN 0-13-170881-3 (student book : bk. 1 : alk. paper) — ISBN 0-13-187490-X (student book : bk. 2 : alk. paper) — ISBN 0-13-194778-8 (student book : bk. 3 : alk. paper) — ISBN 0-13-194784-2 (student book : bk. 4 : alk. paper) 1. English language—Textbooks for foreign speakers. 2. English language—Grammar—Problems, exercises, etc. 3. Vocabulary—Problems, exercises, etc. 4. Life skills—United States. I. Bonesteel, Lynn. II. Eckstut-Didier, Samuela. III. Title.
PE1128.F67425 2007
428.2'4—dc22
                              2006014957

ISBN: 0-13-170881-3

Printed in the United States of America
1 2 3 4 5 6 7 8 9 10-QWD-12 11 10 09 08 07

Acknowledgments

I would like to express my deepest gratitude to all of the staff at Pearson Longman who contributed their creativity and energy to *Center Stage 1*. I especially want to thank editors Margot Gramer and John Barnes for all their invaluable help developing the manuscript and Shelley Gazes for all the care and attention she gave on the production side. Special thanks, too, go to Sherry Preiss and Laura LeDréan for entrusting me with *Center Stage 1*. I would also like to acknowledge Sammi Eckstut-Didier and Lynn Bonesteel for laying the foundation of *Center Stage*.

Heartfelt thanks go to a special group of people who have always cheered me on: my mother, Evelyn Frankel; my father-in-law, Robert Martin; my late mother-in-law, Royal Martin, who almost got to see this book in print; my aunt and uncle, Shirley and Nathan Levine; and my aunt, Hannah Algis. Finally, I want to thank my husband, David Martin, without whose love, support, and understanding I could never have undertaken this project.

Irene Frankel,
author of Student Book 1

The publisher would like to extend special thanks to MaryAnn Florez and Sharon Seymour, our series consultants, and to the following individuals who reviewed the *Center Stage* program and whose comments were instrumental in shaping this series.

Ruth Afifi, Fresno Adult School, Fresno, CA; **Janet L. Barker**, Tarrant Community College, Fort Worth, TX; **Sarah Barnhardt**, Community College of Baltimore County, Baltimore, MD; **Janet Bryant**, Truman College, Chicago, IL; **Rachel Burns**, New England School of English, Cambridge, MA; **Debby Cargill**, Prince William County Public Schools, Manassas, VA; **Veronique Colas**, Los Angeles Technology Center, Los Angeles, CA; **Dave Coleman**, Belmont Community Adult School, Los Angeles, CA; **Eleanor Comegys**, Los Angeles Community Adult School, Los Angeles, CA; **Ludmila Ellis**, Dutchess Community College, Poughkeepsie, NY; **Liz Flynn**, Centers for Education and Technology, San Diego, CA; **Gayle Forgey**, Garden Grove Unified School District, Lincoln Education Center, Garden Grove, CA; **Stephanie Garcia**, Gwinnett Technical College, Lawrenceville, GA; **Jennifer Gaudet**, Santa Ana College, Santa Ana, CA; **Sally Gearhart**, Santa Rosa Junior College, Santa Rosa, CA; **Jeanne Gibson**, Colorado State University, Pueblo, CO; **Anthony Halderman**, Cuesta College, San Luis Obispo, CA; **Cam Tu Huynh**, Banning Adult Learning Center, Los Angeles Unified School District, Los Angeles, CA; **Iordana Iordanova**, Triton College, River Grove, IL; **Mary Jane Jerde**, Prince George's County Adult Education and Howard Community College, Bladensburg, MD; **Britt Johnson**, Albany Park Community Center, Chicago, IL; **Kathleen Krokar**, Truman College, Chicago, IL; **Xay Lee**, Fresno Adult School, Fresno, CA; **Sarah Lynn**, Somerville Community Adult Learning Experiences, Somerville, MA; **Ronna Magy**, Division of Adult and Career Education, LAUSD, Los Angeles, CA; **Dr. Suzanne Medina**, California State University, Carson, CA; **Dr. Diana Mora**, Fresno Adult School, Fresno, CA; **Jenny Moreno**, LAUSD, Los Angeles, CA; **Meg Morris**, Los Altos Adult Education, Mount View, CA; **John Nelson, Ph.D.**, Co-Director ESOL Program, University of Maryland, Baltimore County, MD; **Robert Osgood**, Westchester Community College, Valhalla, NY; **Judie Plumb**, Gwinnett Technical College, Lawrenceville, GA; **Barbara Pongsrikul**, Cesar Chavez Campus, San Diego, CA; **Dr. Yilin Sun**, Seattle Central Community College, Seattle, WA; **Alisa Takeuchi**, Garden Grove Adult Education, Chapman Education Center, Garden Grove, CA; **Garnet Tempin-Ime**, Bellevue Community College, Bellevue, WA; **Lay Kuan Toh**, Westchester Community College, Valhalla, NY; **Marcos Valle**, Edmonds Community College, Edmonds, WA; **Carol van Duzer**, Center for Adult English Language Acquisition, Center for Applied Linguistics, Washington, DC; **Michele Volz**, Centennial Education Center, Santa Ana, CA; **Merari Weber**, Glendale Community College, Glendale, CA.

Scope and Sequence

Unit	Grammar	LIFE SKILLS Listening	Speaking	Reading
1 **It's nice to meet you.** Page 2	*Be*: Affirmative Statements with *Am / Is* Pronouns *He / She* Possessive Adjectives: *His / Her*	Listen to introductions Listen to first and last names and titles Listen to the letters of the alphabet Identify people from conversations	Use *Ms., Miss,* and *Mrs.* Introduce yourself Introduce other people Spell names	Read a personal information form Read for details
2 **Are you from Mexico?** Page 14	*Be*: Statements *Be*: *Yes / No* Questions and Short Answers	Listen to a conversation about a woman's name and nationality Listen to a conversation about foods, countries, and nationalities Identify countries and nationalities Listen for details	Say your nationality and country of origin Interview classmates about their nationalities / countries of origin Ask and answer questions about countries of origin	Read an article about foods and their countries of origin Read for details
3 **Who's he?** Page 26	*A / An* with Singular Nouns *Be*: Information Questions	Listen to a conversation about family members and their occupations Identify people's occupations from a conversation Listen to a conversation about children and their ages Listen for details	Talk about family relationships Describe family members Talk about occupations Talk about people's ages, names, and countries	Read a letter about family members and their occupations Read for details
4 **What's your phone number?** Page 38	Possessive Adjectives Possessive Nouns	Listen to conversations about a phone number and an address Make inferences Listen for details Identify personal information numbers, including phone numbers and street addresses	Talk about phone numbers and e-mail addresses Use *our, your* and *their* to talk about people's names Ask and answer questions about addresses, phone numbers, and e-mail addresses Pronounce final *'s*	Read a personal information form Guess meaning from context

Writing	CASAS	LAUSD Beginning Low	FL. Adult ESOL Low Beginning	Life Skills and Test Prep 1
Prewriting: Write answers to personal information questions Complete a personal information form	0.1.4, 0.2.1 0.1.6 0.1.1, 0.1.2, 0.1.4, 0.1.5, 0.2.1	Competencies: 1, 9b, 9c, 11a, 11b, 58a, 58b 1, 5, 6, 9a, 9b, 9c, 16 Structures: 1a, 9a, 10c, 11a, 16a, c, 19 1a, 9a	2.05.01, 2.15.02, 2.15.05, 2.15.06, 2.16.01, 2.16.02, 2.16.10, 2.16.12, 2.17.01 2.05.01, 2.05.02, 2.16.01, 2.16.02, 2.16.06, 2.16.12, 2.17.01	Unit 1, Lessons 1–3 • Introduce yourself; introduce other people; use titles (*Mr., Ms., Mrs.,* and *Miss*) Unit 2, Lessons 1, 6 • Identify and say letters, spell words; complete forms necessary for everyday activities
Prewriting: Write sentences about national dances Write an article about dances	0.1.2, 0.2.1 0.1.2, 0.1.3, 0.1.4, 0.2.1, 0.2.2, 0.2.4	Competencies: 5 1, 9a, 9b, 9c, 11b, 58a, 58b Structures: 1a, 9a, 9b, 10c, 11a, 14d, 16a, 16c, 19 1a, 9a, 11a	2.01.04, 2.13.03, 2.15.06, 2.16.01, 2.16.02, 2.16.10, 2.16.12, 2.17.01 2.05.01, 2.16.05, 2.16.06, 2.16.08, 2.16.09, 2.16.10, 2.16.12, 2.17.01	Unit 1, Lessons 2, 5 • Introduce other people; ask where people are from
Prewriting: Answer questions about family and friends Write a letter about family and friends	0.1.2, 0.2.1, 0.2.4, 4.1.8 0.1.2, 0.1.5, 2.2.1, 4.1.8	Competencies: 3, 6, 13, 50 12, 50 Structures: 1a, 9, 10a, 10c, 10d, 11a, 14d, 16a, 16c, 19 1a, 5, 9a, 9c, 10a, 10c, 10d, 11a, 14a, 15a, 16a, 16c	2.01.04, 2.05.01, 2.05.02, 2.14.01, 2.15.06, 2.16.01, 2.16.02, 2.16.05, 2.16.06, 2.16.09, 2.16.10, 2.16.12, 2.17.01 2.05.01, 2.14.01, 2.16.01, 2.16.02, 2.16.05, 2.16.10, 2.16.12, 2.17.01	Unit 1, Lesson 4 • Identify family members Unit 2, Lesson 2 • Count and use numbers 0-9 in daily life Unit 12, Lesson 1 • Identify common occupations
Prewriting: Answer questions about your name, address, and phone number Complete a personal information form	0.1.2, 0.2.1, 0.2.2, 0.2.4 0.1.2, 0.1.4, 0.2.1, 2.4.1	Competencies: 1, 2, 3, 4, 5, 6, 7, 13 2, 5, 6, 7, 8 Structures: 1a, 7, 9a, 11a, 12a, 16a, 16c, 19 1a, 9a, 10a, 10c, 11a, 12a, 13a, 14c, 16a, 16c	2.05.01, 2.05.02, 2.15.05, 2.15.06, 2.16.01, 2.16.02, 2.16.05, 2.16.08, 2.16.10, 2.16.11, 2.16.12, 2.17.01, 2.17.02 2.05.01, 2.08.01, 2.16.01, 2.16.02, 2.16.05, 2.16.12, 2.17.01	Unit 1, Lessons 4–5 • Identify family members; ask where people are from Unit 2, Lessons 2–4, 6 • Count and use numbers 0-9 in daily life; count and use numbers 10-100 in daily life; say and write addresses; complete forms necessary for everyday activities

All information printed in red pertains to *Life Skills and Test Prep 1*

Writing	CASAS	LAUSD Beginning Low	FL. Adult ESOL Low Beginning	Life Skills and Test Prep 1
Prewriting: Complete the personal information section of a test application form Complete a test application form	0.1.2, 0.1.5, 0.1.6, 0.2.1, 0.2.2, 0.2.4, 7.4.7 0.1.2, 0.1.5, 5.3.1	Competencies: 2, 4, 7, 11a, 11b, 11c, 12 , 15, 18, 59b 1, 2, 3, 4, 5, 7, 9d, 10, 11a, 12, 15 Structures: 1a, 5, 9, 10a, 10c, 11a, 12a, 14a, 16a, 16c, 19 1a, 9a, 10a, 11a, 14b, 14c, 16a, 16c, 17	2.05.01, 2.15.05, 2.15.06, 2.16.01, 2.16.02, 2.16.05, 2.16.06, 2.16.08, 2.16.09, 2.16.10, 2.16.11, 2.16.12, 2.17.01 2.05.01, 2.16.01, 2.16.02, 2.16.05, 2.16.08, 2.16.09, 2.16.12, 2.17.01	Unit 3, Lesson 1 • Identify classroom objects; give and follow simple instructions Unit 2, Lesson 6 • Complete forms necessary for everyday activities
Prewriting: Answer questions about your family's schedules Write an e-mail about the schedules of people in your household	0.1.4, 0.2.4, 1.1.5, 2.3.1, 2.3.3 0.1.2, 0.1.6, 0.2.1, 2.3.1, 2.3.2, 2.3.3, 4.4.3, 6.0.1, 6.0.2	Competencies: 9, 13, 14a, 25, 28, 29 9d, 11b, 25, 26, 28, 29, 55 Structures: 1a, 9a, 9b, 9c, 9d, 10a, 10b, 10c, 10d, 11a, 12a, 13a, 14c, 16a, 16c, 19 1a, 1b, 2, 9a, 9b, 9d, 10a, 10b, 11a, 12a, 12b, 14a, 16a, 16c, 19, 20	2.02.04, 2.05.01, 2.05.03, 2.08.02, 2.08.03, 2.11.01, 2.11.03 , 2.11.04, 2.13.01, 2.15.06, 2.16.01 , 2.16.02, 2.16.04 , 2.16.05, 2.16.06 , 2.16.07, 2.16.08, 2.17.01, 2.17.02 2.05.01, 2.08.01, 2.08.03, 2.16.01, 2.16.02, 2.16.04, 2.16.05, 2.16.07, 2.16.08, 2.16.09, 2.16.12, 2.17.01	Unit 4, Lessons 1–3, 7 • Read time and ask for the time; identify and spell the days of the week; use the months of the year and their abbreviations; use the seasons of the year; talk about the weather Unit 12, Lesson 5 • Read a work schedule
Prewriting: Choose the color, size, item number, and price of clothes from a mail-order catalog Complete an order form	0.1.2, 0.2.4, 1.1.6, 1.1.9, 1.2.1, 1.2.3, 1.2.5, 1.3.4, 1.3.7, 1.3.9, 2.2.1, 6.0.1, 6.0.2, 6.5.1 0.1.2, 0.1.3, 0.1.4, 0.1.6, 0.2.1, 1.1.6, 1.1.9, 1.3.9, 6.0.1, 6.0.2, 6.5.1	Competencies: 13, 14a, 30, 31, 32, 33, 34 9a, 9d, 11a, 11b, 14a, 30a, 30b, 33, 34 Structures: 1a, 9, 10a, 10b, 10c, 10d, 10e, 11a, 12a, 12, 14a, 16a, 16c, 19 1a, 1b, 8, 9a, 9b, 9d, 10a, 11a, 16a, 16c, 19, 20	2.05.03, 2.08.01, 2.08.04, 2.08.05, 2.11.01, 2.11.03, 2.11.04, 2.15.01, 2.15.05, 2.15.06, 2.16.01, 2.16.02, 2.16.04, 2.16.05, 2.16.07, 2.16.08, 2.16.09, 2.16.10, 2.16.11, 2.16.12, 2.17.01, 2.17.02 2.11.01, 2.11.03, 2.11.04, 2.16.01, 2.16.02, 2.16.05, 2.16.07, 2.16.08, 2.16.09, 2.16.12, 1.17.01	Unit 6, Lessons 2–5 • Read simple receipts; identify different types of clothing; talk about clothing sizes; ask for and give prices Unit 2, Lesson 6 • Complete forms necessary for everyday activities
Prewriting: Write an ad for your perfect apartment Answer questions about a perfect apartment Write an e-mail describing a perfect apartment	0.1.2, 0.1.6, 1.1.6, 1.4.1, 1.4.2, 2.2.1, 2.6.4, 3.5.2, 3.5.9, 6.6.5, 7.3.1 0.1.2, 0.1.3, 0.1.4, 1.4.1, 1.4.2	Competencies: 23, 38, 39 12, 13, 38, 39 Structures: 1a, 9, 10a, 10c, 11a, 12a, 12b, 13b, 14a, 16a, 16c, 19 1a, 1b, 1c, 2, 9a, 9b, 9c, 9d, 10a, 11a, 12a, 12b, 13b, 14a, 16a, 16c, 19, 20	2.05.03, 2.11.06, 2.11.08, 2.15.06, 2.16.01, 2.16.02, 2.16.05, 2.16.06, 2.16.07, 2.16.08, 2.16.09, 2.16.10, 2.16.12 2.05.01, 2.05.03, 2.11.06, 2.11.08, 2.16.01, 2.16.02, 2.16.05, 2.16.07, 2.16.08, 2.16.09, 2.16.12, 1.17.01	Unit 8, Lessons 1–2, 4 • Identify rooms of a house; identify words for furniture; understand apartment ads, including abbreviations

All information printed in red pertains to *Life Skills and Test Prep 1*

Writing	CASAS	LAUSD Beginning Low	FL. Adult ESOL Low Beginning	*Life Skills and Test Prep 1*
Write a letter about two problem eaters	0.1.2, 0.1.3, 1.1.6, 1.2.1, 2.6.4 0.1.2, 0.1.3, 0.1.4, 0.1.6, 0.1.7, 0.2.1, 1.3.8, 2.6.4, 6.0.1, 6.0.2	Competencies: 9d, 14a, 30, 31, 37 9d, 14a, 30, 31, 35, 36, 37 Structures: 1a, 1b, 1c, 9, 10a, 10b, 10c, 10d, 11a, 12a, 12b, 16a, 16b, 16c, 17, 18, 19 1a, 1b, 8, 9b, 9d, 10a, 11a, 16a, 16c, 18, 19, 20	2.05.01, 2.05.03, 2.07.10, 2.07.11, 2.08.04, 2.11.01, 2.15.06, 2.16.01, 2.16.02, 2.16.05, 2.16.06, 2.16.07, 2.16.08, 2.16.09, 2.16.12, 2.17.01 2.05.01, 2.05.03, 2.07.11, 2.8.04, 2.11.01, 2.11.02, 2.16.01, 2.16.02, 2.16.05, 2.16.06, 2.16.07, 2.16.08, 2.16.09, 2.16.12, 2.17.01	Unit 7, Lessons 1–2, 4 • Identify different foods; express likes and dislikes; use words for food containers and quantities; order in a restaurant
Prewriting: Answer questions about personal information Complete a patient information form	0.1.2, 0.1.4, 0.2.1, 0.2.2, 0.2.4, 3.1.1, 3.2.1, 3.3.1, 3.3.3, 3.5.9, 7.3.1, 7.3.2 0.1.2, 0.1.3, 0.1.4, 0.2.1, 2.3.1, 2.3.2, 3.1.1, 3.1.2, 3.1.3	Competencies: 1, 2, 3, 7, 9, 11, 13, 43, 44, 45, 46 24, 26, 27, 43, 44, 46 Structures: 1a,1b, 5, 9, 10a, 10b, 10c, 11a, 12a, 12b, 16a, 16c, 17, 19 1a, 1b, 5, 10a, 10c, 10d, 11a, 14a, 16c, 18	2.01.04, 2.05.03, 2.07.01, 2.07.02, 2.07.03, 2.07.06, 2.15.05, 2.15.06, 2.16.01, 2.16.02, 2.16.04, 2.16.05, 2.16.06, 2.16.07, 2.16.08, 2.16.09, 2.16.10, 2.16.12, 2.17.01, 2.17.02 2.05.01, 2.07.01, 2.07.02, 2.07.03, 2.07.04, 2.07.05, 2.08.01, 2.08.02, 2.08.03, 2.15.05, 2.16.01, 2.16.02, 2.16.05, 2.16.07, 2.16.08, 2.16.09, 2.16.12, 2.17.01	Unit 10, Lessons 1–2, 4 • Identify parts of the body; talk about aches and pains; follow doctor's instructions Unit 2, Lesson 6 Complete forms necessary for everyday activities
Prewriting: Do a class survey about breakfast routines and make a graph based on the survey Write sentences about the survey	0.1.2, 0.2.1, 0.2.2, 0.2.4, 2.1.8, 3.5.9, 6.7.2, 7.1.1, 7.2.1, 7.2.2, 7.2.3, 7.2.4, 7.4.8, 8.2.2 0.1.2, 0.2.1, 0.2.2, 0.2.4, 1.8.2, 8.2.1, 8.2.2, 8.2.3, 8.2.4	Competencies: 6, 7, 9a, 12, 14a, 19, 20, 60 7, 12, 13 Structures: 1 a, 1b, 1c, 9, 10a, 10b, 10c, 11a, 12a, 12b, 15d, 16a, 16c, 17, 19 1c, 2, 9b, 9c, 10a, 11a, 16c	2.05.01, 2.05.02, 2.05.03, 2.06.01, 2.07.10, 2.15.05, 2.15.06, 2.16.01, 2.16.02, 2.16.03, 2.16.04, 2.16.05, 2.16.06, 2.16.07, 2.16.08, 2.16.09, 2.16.10, 2.16.12, 2.17.01, 2.17.02 2.05.02, 2.08.05, 2.15.05, 2.16.01, 2.16.02, 2.16.05, 2.16.06, 2.16.08, 2.16.09, 2.16.11, 2.16.12, 2.17.01	Unit 8, Lesson 3 • Talk about different activities at home
Prewriting: Draw a neighborhood map Write an e-mail about a neighborhood	0.1.2, 0.1.4, 0.1.6, 0.2.1, 2.2.1, 0.2.2, 0.2.3, 0.2.4, 2.5.1, 2.5.3, 2.5.5 0.1.2, 0.1.4, 0.2.1, 0.2.4, 1.3.8, 2.2.1, 2.2.3, 2.2.5	Competencies: 7, 9a, 9d, 11a, 11b, 11c, 13, 14a, 22, 23a, 23b 9d, 11a, 22, 23a, 23b, 24a, 14a, 35 Structures: 1a, 1b, 9, 10a, 10b, 10c, 11a, 11b, 12a, 12b, 13b, 14a, 16a, 16c, 17, 19 1a, 1b, 9a, 9b, 9d, 10a, 11a, 14a, 16a, 16c, 19	2.05.01, 2.05.03, 2.07.10, 2.09.04, 2.12.01, 2.12.02, 2.15.05, 2.15.06, 2.16.01, 2.16.02, 2.16.03, 2.16.04, 2.16.05, 2.16.06, 2.16.07, 2.16.08, 2.16.09, 2.16.10, 2.16.12, 2.17.01 2.05.01, 2.05.03, 2.07.09, 2.09.04, 2.12.01, 2.12.02, 2.12.03, 2.16.01, 2.16.02, 2.16.05, 2.16.08, 2.16.09, 2.16.12, 2.17.01	Unit 5, Lessons 1–2 • Name different places in the community; read a map and ask for locations; identify different kinds of transportation Unit 7, Lesson 1 • Identify different foods

All information printed in red pertains to *Life Skills and Test Prep 1*

Unit	Grammar	Listening	Speaking	Reading
13 I'm talking on the phone. Page 146	Present Progressive: Affirmative Statements Present Progressive: Negative Statements	Listen to conversations about people's activities Identify what people are doing Listen for details	Talk about leisure activities Ask and answer about ongoing activities Talk about household chores Understand home-care skills	Read an e-mail about people's activities Scan for details
14 Are you walking to school? Page 158	Present Progressive: *Yes / No* Questions and Short Answers Present Progressive: Information Questions	Listen to conversations about forms of transportation Listen to a conversation between two police officers following a car Understand directions Listen for details	Talk about forms of transportation Ask and answer questions about the forms of transportation people are using Ask and answer questions about what people are doing	Read an e-mail describing ongoing activities Scan for details
15 My boyfriend can't sing. Page 170	*Can* for Ability: Statements *Can* for Ability: *Yes / No* Questions *Can* for Ability: Information Questions	Listen to a conversation about a person's talents and abilities Listen to a conversation about qualifications needed for a job Listen for details	Ask and answer questions about hobbies Talk about people's talents and abilities Talk about workplaces and job requirements Ask and answer questions about people's abilities and job possibilities	Read job ads Read for details Understand how to find and apply for a job Understand basic duties of common occupations
16 We were at home. Page 182	Simple Past of *Be*: Statements Simple Past of *Be*: *Yes / No* Questions and Short Answers Simple Past of *Be*: Wh-Questions	Listen to a conversation about a wedding Listen to conversations about a vacation Listen for details	Ask and answer questions about favorite places Talk about recent weekend activities Talk about the weather Talk about birthdays and other important events Ask and answer questions about past events	Understand daily planners Read a list of U.S. bank holidays Identify national holidays Understand dates Scan for details

Writing	CASAS	LAUSD Beginning Low	FL. Adult ESOL Low Beginning	Life Skills and Test Prep 1
Prewriting: Write sentences about people's activities Write an e-mail about people's activities	0.1.2, 0.1.4, 0.2.1, 0.2.3, 0.2.4, 2.6.1, 8.2.1, 8.2.2, 8.2.3, 8.2.4, 8.2.5, 8.2.6, 8.3.1 0.1.2, 0.2.1, 0.2.2, 0.2.4, 1.8.2, 8.2.1, 8.2.2, 8.2.3, 8.2.4	Competencies: 9a, 9b, 9d, 12, 13 7, 12, 13 Structures: 1a, 1b, 1c, 2, 9, 10a, 10c, 11a, 12a, 12b, 14a, 15d, 16a, 16c, 17, 19, 20 1c, 2, 9b, 9c, 10a, 11a, 16c	2.05.01, 2.05.02, 2.05.03, 2.06.01, 2.15.06, 2.16.01, 2.16.02, 2.16.03, 2.16.05, 2.16.06, 2.16.07, 2.16.08, 2.16.09, 2.16.10, 2.16.12, 2.17.01 2.05.02, 2.08.05, 2.15.05, 2.16.01, 2.16.02, 2.16.05, 2.16.06, 2.16.08, 2.16.09, 2.16.11, 2.16.12, 2.17.01	Unit 8, Lesson 3 • Talk about different activities at home
Prewriting: Draw a picture showing what people are doing on a busy street Write an e-mail about what people are doing in the picture	0.1.2, 0.1.4, 0.2.4, 1.1.3, 2.2.1, 2.2.2, 2.2.3, 2.5.1, 2.5.3, 3.4.2, 3.5.9 0.1.2, 0.2.1, 0.2.4, 1.9.1, 2.2.2, 2.2.3	Competencies: 9a, 9d, 22, 23b, 24a 13, 24 Structures 1a, 1b, 2, 5, 9, 10a, 10b, 10c, 11a, 12a, 12b, 13a, 13b, 14b, 16a, 16c, 19 1b, 10a, 11a, 14a	2.05.01, 2.09.01, 2.09.02, 2.09.03, 2.09.04, 2.15.06, 2.16.01, 2.16.02, 2.16.05, 2.16.07, 2.16.08, 2.16.09, 2.16.10, 2.16.11, 2.16.12, 2.17.01 2.05.0, 2.09.01, 2.15.05, 2.16.01, 2.16.02, 2.16.05, 2.16.08, 2.16.09, 2.17.01	Unit 5, Lessons 2, 5 • Identify different kinds of transportation; read simple highway and street signs
Prewriting: Match a job application with the appropriate ad Complete a job application form	0.1.2, 0.1.4, 0.2.1, 0.2.2, 0.2.4, 4.1.2, 4.1.3, 4.1.5, 4.1.6, 4.1.8, 4.4.2 0.1.2, 0.1.3, 0.1.4, 0.2.1, 0.2.2, 0.2.4, 1.8.2, 2.2.1, 2.2.3, 2.2.5, 4.1.2, 4.1.3, 4.1.6, 4.1.8, 4.4.3, 4.4.4, 8.2.1, 8.2.2, 8.2.3, 8.2.4	Competencies: 7, 9a, 12, 13, 14, 50, 52, 54, 55 7, 13, 22, 50, 51, 52, 55 Structures: 1a,1b,1c, 2, 6, 9, 10a, 10c, 11a, 12a, 12b, 14a, 14c, 16a, 16c, 17, 19 1a, 1c, 9, 10a, 11a, 14a, 14c, 16a, 16c, 19	2.01.01, 2.01.02, 2.01.03, 2.01.04, 2.02.01, 2.05.01, 2.05.03, 2.15.05, 2.15.06, 2.16.01, 2.16.02, 2.16.04, 2.16.05, 2.16.06, 2.16.07, 2.16.08, 2.16.09, 2.16.10, 2.16.12, 2.17.01 2.01.01, 2.01.02, 2.01.03, 2.02.04, 2.05.02, 2.08.05, 2.15.05, 2.16.01, 2.16.02, 2.16.05, 2.16.06, 2.16.08, 2.16.09, 2.16.11, 2.16.12, 2.17.01	Unit 5, Lesson 1 • Name different places in the community Unit 8, Lesson 3 • Talk about different activities at home Unit 12, Lessons 1–3, 5 • Identify common occupations; describe what people do in their jobs; read and understand job ads; read a work schedule Unit 2, Lesson 6 • Complete forms necessary for everyday activities
Prewriting: Use abbreviations to write the dates of holidays Write dates in three different ways Understand cardinal and ordinal numbers	0.1.3, 0.1.4, 0.2.1, 0.2.4, 2.3.2, 2.3.3, 2.6.1, 2.6.3, 2.7.1, 3.1.2 0.1.2, 0.1.4, 0.2.1, 2.3.2, 2.3.3, 2.7.1	Competencies: 9a, 12, 13, 14, 26, 28, 40 3, 13, 17, 40 Structures: 1a, 1b, 1c, 2, 4a, 9, 10a, 10b, 10c, 10d, 11a, 12a, 12b, 13a, 13b, 14a, 14b, 14c, 15a, 15b, 15d, 16a, 16c, 17, 19 1a, 9a, 9b, 9c, 9d, 10a, 10c, 11a, 12a, 16a, 16c, 19	2.05.01, 2.05.02, 2.05.03, 2.08.01, 2.08.02, 2.08.03, 2.15.05, 2.15.06, 2.16.01, 2.16.02, 2.16.03, 2.16.04, 2.16.05, 2.16.06, 2.16.07, 2.16.08, 2.16.09, 2.16.10, 2.16.11, 2.16.12, 2.17.01, 2.17.02 2.05.01, 2.05.02, 2.05.03, 2.08.01, 2.08.03, 2.13.01, 2.16.01, 2.16.02, 2.16.05, 2.16.08, 2.16.09, 2.16.10, 2.16.12, 2.17.01	Unit 3, Lessons 3–4 • Use ordinal numbers Unit 4, Lessons 4–6 • Read, write, and say the dates; recognize dates of major holidays; talk about the weather

All information printed in red pertains to *Life Skills and Test Prep 1*

To the Teacher

Center Stage is a four-level, four-skills course that supports student learning and achievement in everyday work and life situations. Practical language and timely topics motivate adult students to master grammar along with speaking, listening, reading, and writing skills.

Features

- *Grammar to Communicate* presents key grammar points with concise charts and abundant practice in real-life situations.

- **Communicative activities**, such as *Time to Talk*, promote opportunities for meaningful expression and active learning.

- Extensive **listening** practice, in addition to **reading** and **writing** activities, helps students to master the English they need in their daily lives.

- *Review* lessons help teachers to assess students' progress and meet the needs of multi-level classrooms.

- Easy-to-follow, **two-page lessons** give students a sense of accomplishment.

Additional Components

- A **companion student book**, *Life Skills and Test Prep 1*, provides thorough practice of life skills and is linked to the unit themes and vocabulary of *Center Stage*.

- The **Teacher's Edition** includes unit tests, multi-level strategies, learner persistence tips, expansion activities, culture, grammar and language notes, and answer keys.

- A **Teacher's Resource Disk**, in the back of the Teacher's Edition, offers numerous worksheets for supplementary grammar practice, supplementary vocabulary practice, and learner persistence.

- **Color transparencies** provide an ideal resource for introducing, practicing, and reviewing vocabulary.

- The **Audio Program** contains recordings for all listening and pronunciation activities in the Student Book.

- The *ExamView® Assessment Suite* includes hundreds of test items, providing flexible, comprehensive assessment.

Unit Description

Each of the sixteen units centers on practical themes for the adult learner. A unit consists of 12 pages and is divided into the following lessons: *Vocabulary and Listening 1*, *Grammar to Communicate 1*, *Vocabulary and Listening 2*, *Grammar to Communicate 2*, *Reading and Writing*, and *Review*.

Each lesson is presented on two facing pages and provides clear, self-contained instruction that takes approximately 45 to 60 minutes of class time.

Vocabulary and Listening

Each unit has eye-catching illustrations that set the context and present high frequency, leveled vocabulary that is recycled in the unit and throughout the course. After hearing the new words, students listen to a dialogue related to the unit theme. In the dialogue, students hear the grammar for the unit before it is formally presented. Students listen for meaning and check their comprehension in follow-up exercises.

Grammar to Communicate

Each unit has two *Grammar to Communicate* lessons that present target structures in concise charts. Students practice each language point through a variety of exercises that build from controlled to open-ended. Extensive meaningful practice leads students toward mastery.

> **Look Boxes.** Lessons are often expanded with tips in *Look Boxes*. These tips provide information on usage, pronunciation, and spelling.

> **Time to Talk.** *Grammar to Communicate* culminates with a *Time to Talk* activity. This highly communicative activity gives students the chance to personalize what they have learned.

Reading and Writing

A reading and writing lesson follows the second *Grammar to Communicate* lesson in each unit.

> **Reading.** The reading lesson recycles the grammar and vocabulary that have been taught in the unit. The reading selections include practical documents such as e-mails and letters. Students read for general meaning. Comprehension questions build reading skills such as recognizing the main idea and scanning for details. The reading selections also encourage students to read for life skills, for example, interpreting a personal information form.

> **Writing.** The writing lesson begins with a prewriting activity that prepares students for the main writing task. These tasks range from filling out forms, to writing e-mails, to writing letters. For each assignment, students are given a model to guide their writing.

Review

Each unit concludes with a *Review* lesson which helps students review the unit material and consolidate their knowledge. *Review* includes:

> **Put It in Place.** This section offers a brief review of the target grammar presented in the unit.

> **Put It Together.** Colorfully illustrated games are a unique feature of *Center Stage*. The Games review the grammar and vocabulary from the unit in a light and communicative context. The Games motivate students to practice the language in a relaxed situation.

Beyond the Unit

There are a number of supplementary resources in the back of the book. In addition to a complete map of the United States and Canada and a map of the world, there are the following materials:

Pronunciation Activities

For each unit of the book, there are two pronunciation exercises that focus on key points related to vocabulary or grammar. Students hear examples of the point, do an exercise to demonstrate their understanding, and practice speaking. Cross-references to these exercises are on the appropriate student book page.

Spelling Rules

Rules that relate to specific grammar points are summarized in chart form. Cross-references to these rules appear near the grammar charts within the units.

Capitalization and Punctuation Rules

Relevant rules for capitalization and punctuation provide support for the writing exercises in each unit.

How to Play the Games

Each unit ends with a game or information gap activity that allows students to review the vocabulary and grammar in a fun, interactive way. Simplified instructions for these activities appear in the unit; full versions of the instructions appear in the back of the book.

Audioscript

The audioscript includes all the recorded material that is not on the student book page.

Standards and Assessment

Standards. Meeting national and state standards is critical to successful adult instruction. *Center Stage 1,* together with the companion text, *Life Skills and Test Prep 1,* integrates material from key grammar and life skills standards. The scope and sequence on pages iv–xi links the two books with the corresponding standards.

Assessment. *Center Stage* also includes several assessment tools. Teachers have multiple opportunities for performance-based assessment on productive tasks using the 32 *Time to Talk* communicative activities. In addition, students have many opportunities for self-assessment in the *Review* section.

The testing material for *Center Stage* includes end-of-unit tests found in the *Teacher's Edition.* In addition, the *ExamView® Assessment Suite* includes hundreds of test items for each Student Book. The *Life Skills and Test Prep 1* companion book features CASAS-style unit tests.

Life Skills and Test Prep 1

Life Skills and Test Prep 1 gives teachers the flexibility to teach additional life skills topics and test-taking tips and practice based on student needs. The 60 lessons, correlated to CASAS competencies, allow teachers and students to choose among many topics—from family and school, and finding a job, to giving personal information and health. This competency-based, multiple skills student book prepares students for any standards-based test. *Life Skills and Test Prep 1* has a separate audio program and Teacher's Manual. The *Center Stage Teacher's Edition* provides specific point-of-use cross references to the lessons in *Life Skills and Test Prep 1.*

About the Author

Irene Frankel has been a teacher and administrator in both adult ESL and EFL programs for more than 20 years. She has done extensive teacher training, in particular, helping teachers to work with multilevel classes and develop their classroom management skills. Ms. Frankel is the co-author of numerous adult ESL and EFL student books, workbooks, and teacher's editions. As a publisher, she has been responsible for a variety of successful courses, including *Longman English Interactive*; *WorldView*; *Longman ESL Literacy*, Third Edition; and *Life Skills and Test Prep*. Ms. Frankel holds an M.A. in TESOL from New York University.

About the Series Consultants

MaryAnn Florez is the lead ESL Specialist for the Arlington Education and Employment Program (REEP) in Arlington, Virginia, where she has program management, curriculum development, and teacher training responsibilities. She has worked with Fairfax County (VA) Adult ESOL and the National Center for ESL Literacy Education (NCLE), and has coordinated a volunteer adult ESL program in Northern Virginia. Ms. Florez has offered workshops throughout the U.S. in areas such as teaching beginning level English language learners, incorporating technology in instruction, strategies for a multi-level classroom, and assessment. Her publications include a variety of research-to-practice briefs and articles on adult ESL education. Ms. Florez holds an M.Ed. in Adult Education from George Mason University.

Sharon Seymour is an ESL instructor at City College of San Francisco, where she has extensive experience teaching both noncredit adult ESL and credit ESL. She recently completed ten years as chair of the ESL Department at CCSF. She is also currently a co-researcher for a Center for Advancement of Adult Literacy Project on Exemplary Noncredit Community College ESL Programs. Ms. Seymour has been president of CATESOL and a member of the TESOL board of directors and has served both organizations in a variety of capacities. She has served on California Community College Chancellor's Office and California State Department of Education committees relating to ESL curriculum and assessment. Ms. Seymour holds an M.A. in TESOL from San Francisco State University.

Welcome to *Center Stage*

Center Stage is a four-level, four-skills course that supports student learning and achievement in everyday work and life situations. Practical language and timely topics motivate adult students to master grammar along with speaking, listening, reading, and writing skills.

Target grammar is clearly defined at the start of the unit.

Students listen for general comprehension and details in real life contexts.

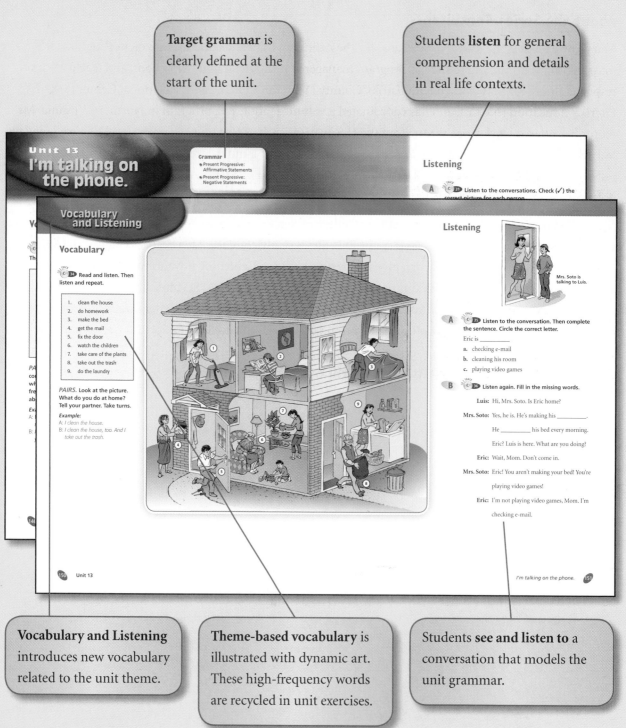

Vocabulary and Listening introduces new vocabulary related to the unit theme.

Theme-based vocabulary is illustrated with dynamic art. These high-frequency words are recycled in unit exercises.

Students see and listen to a conversation that models the unit grammar.

Each unit has two **Grammar to Communicate** lessons that present the target grammar in a clear and concise chart followed by practice exercises.

Look Boxes expand on the *Grammar to Communicate* charts and include usage information, tips on pronunciation, and spelling notes.

Grammar to Communicate 2

IMPERATIVES

Affirmative		Negative			Contraction
Verb		Do + Not	Verb		Do + not → Don't
Open Close	the door. the window. your books.	Do not	open close	the door. the window. your books.	

A Look at the pictures. Check (✓) the correct response.

1.

Look

Use *please* with the imperative to be polite.
Please open the door.
Please close the window.

B Look at the verbs on the left. Each verb goes with one pair of phrases on the right. Match the verbs on the left with the phrases on the right.

_e_	1. turn to	a.	sentence number 5 / a book
___	2. read	b.	the board / the mistake
___	3. take out	c.	your name / the answers
___	4. listen to	d.	the door / your book
___	5. open	e.	page 48 / your partner
___	6. write	f.	a pen / your workbook
___	7. erase	g.	the CD / your teacher

C Complete the sentences. Write affirmative or negative imperatives. Use the verbs in parentheses. Sometimes you will need to use a capital letter.

1. Please ___don't write___ on the test.
   (not write)

2. Please _____ your hand to answer.
   (raise)

3. _____ your partner's answers, please.

Grammar to Communicate 1

PLURAL OF REGULAR NOUNS

Singular		Plural		Singular			Plural		
a	book	two	books	The book			The books		
a	pen	three	pens	The pen			The pens		
an	eraser	many	erasers	The eraser	is	here.	The erasers	are	here.
a	student		students	The student			The students		

A Choose the correct word. Write it on the line.

1. Where are the ___books___ ?
   (book / books)

2. Is this your _____ ?
   (pen / pens)

3. Andrea's _____ is on her desk.
   (dictionary / dictionaries)

4. The _____ is on the bookcase.
   (notebook / notebooks)

5. The _____ are in the box.
   (pencil / pencils)

6. Where are the _____ ?
   (eraser / erasers)

7. The _____ is near the door.
   (bookcase / bookcases)

Look

a dictionary   two dictionaries
a box   two boxes

For spelling rules of plural nouns, see page 213.

B Rewrite the sentences. Change the underlined words to the plural. Make all necessary changes.

1. Please open the box.   Please open the boxes.
2. Let's go over the answer. _____
3. Where is the dictionary? _____
4. Dan's book is on his desk. _____
5. The closet door is open. _____
6. The window isn't open. _____
7. Teresa's pencil is in her backpack. _____

C Complete the questions. Look at the pictures. Answer the questions. Use *on* and *in*.

1. A: Where _are the books?_
   B: _They're in the closet._

2. A: Where _____
   B: _____

3. A: Where _____
   B: _____

4. A: Where _____
   B: _____

5. A: Where _____
   B: _____

D 🎧 Listen and check your answers.

PAIRS. Practice the conversations in Exercise C.

TIME TO TALK

GROUPS. Each student, guess: How many books are in your group? How many pens? How many pencils? How many dictionaries? How many backpacks? Write your guesses.

Compare your answers.

Count how many books, pens, pencils, dictionaries, and backpacks you have in your group. Write the numbers. Are you right?

See Pronunciation Activity A: page 201

Open your books.   53

Grammar practice exercises build from controlled to open-ended.

Each grammar presentation ends with **Time to Talk**, an activity that motivates students to apply what they have learned in meaningful exchanges.

Prewriting activities prepare students for the writing task.

Reading features practical documents and practices essential reading skills.

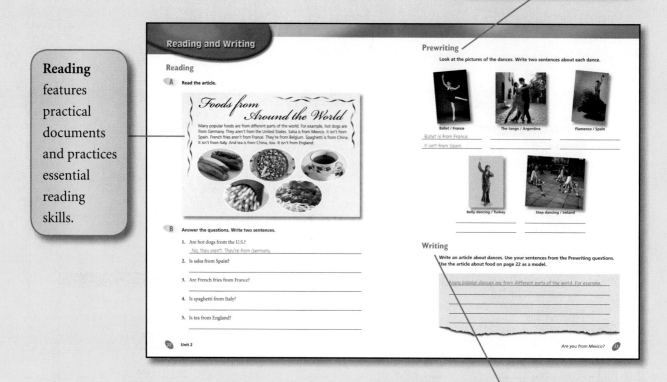

Review reviews and consolidates the *Grammar to Communicate* lessons.

Writing guides students to complete the writing task with clear, controlled models.

Colorful, fun **Games** provide opportunities for self-assessment as well as grammar and vocabulary review.

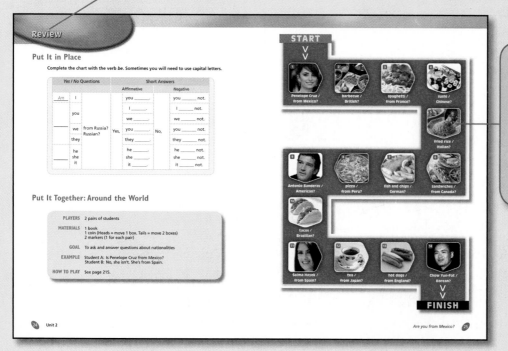

Beyond the Unit

The page numbers for relevant *Pronunciation Activities* are given at the bottom of appropriate pages in the lessons.

Each **Pronunciation Activity** begins with a short audio excerpt to illustrate the pronunciation point taught.

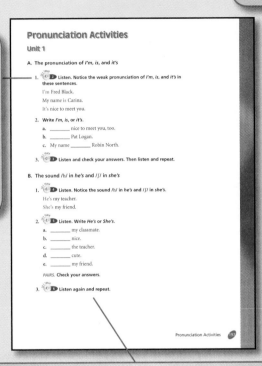

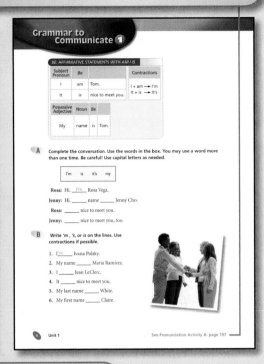

Students **practice** the pronunciation point in natural contexts, **demonstrate** their understanding, and **repeat** examples to reinforce what they have learned.

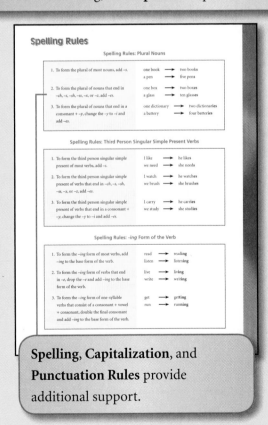

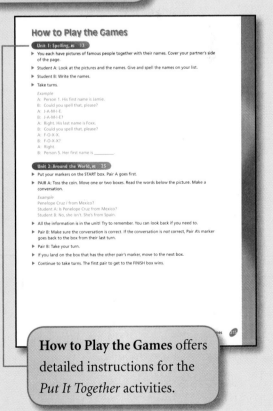

Spelling, Capitalization, and **Punctuation Rules** provide additional support.

How to Play the Games offers detailed instructions for the *Put It Together* activities.

Teaching Support

The *Center Stage Teacher's Edition* features learning goals, learner persistence tips, step-by-step teaching notes, expansion activities, multi-level strategies, unit tests, and answer keys. The accompanying **Teacher's Resource Disk** includes supplementary grammar and vocabulary exercises and learner persistence worksheets.

Learner persistence tips introduce techniques to engage and retain students and help teachers adapt to a variety of student needs.

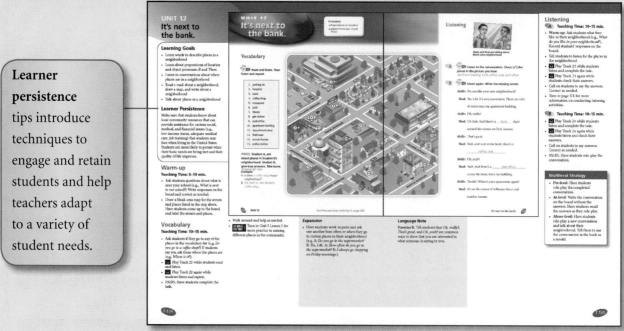

Clear links to the *Life Skills and Test Prep 1* companion book are provided.

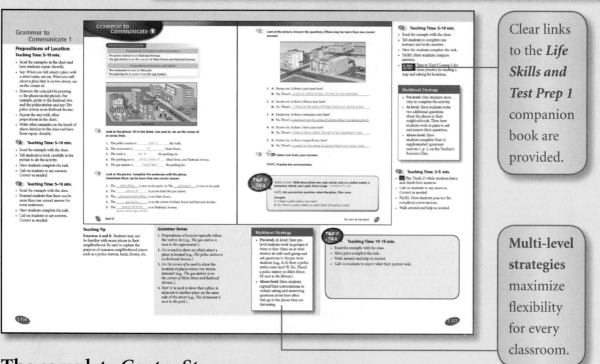

Multi-level strategies maximize flexibility for every classroom.

The complete *Center Stage* program

- Audio program
- *ExamView® Assessment Suite*
- Transparencies
- Companion Website

Life Skills and Test Prep 1

Life Skills and Test Prep 1, a companion book, provides instruction in the life skills competencies that adult students need at home, at work, and in their communities.

Each lesson features extensive practice in **listening, speaking, reading, and writing.**

A total of **60 life skills** lessons are correlated to key CASAS competencies.

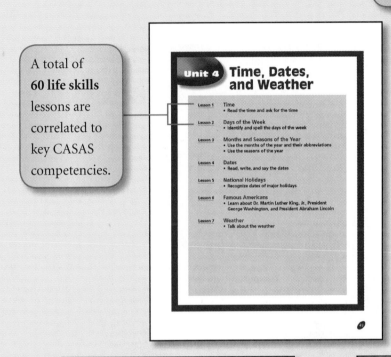

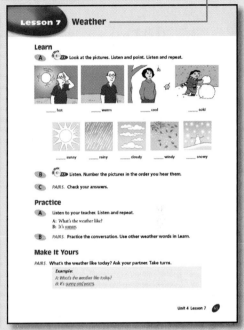

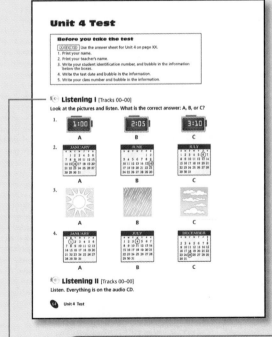

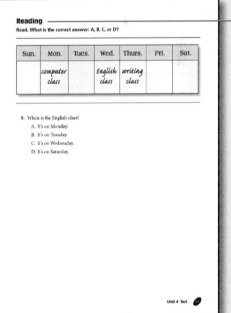

Each unit has **listening and reading tests** with perforated bubble-in answer sheets. The tests assess mastery of the competencies as well as provide essential practice in taking standardized tests.

Tour of the Program

xxi

Unit 1

It's nice to meet you.

Grammar
- *Be:* Affirmative Statements with *Am* / *Is*
- Pronouns *He* / *She*
- Possessive Adjectives: *His* / *Her*

Vocabulary

CD 1 TRACK **2** **Read and listen. Then listen and repeat.**

first name
last name
family name
Mr. *(Mister)*
Ms. *(Miz)*

Look

First name = Tom
Last name
Family name } = Bailey
Men use *Mr.* + last name
Example: Mr. Bailey
Mr. = Mister

First name = Norma
Last name
Family name } = Sanchez
Women use *Ms.* + last name
Example: Ms. Sanchez

PAIRS. **Look at the picture. Student A, say a name. Use *Mr.* and *Ms.*, for example, *Mr. Charles.* Student B, point to the person. Take turns.**

2   Unit 1

Listening

A CD 1 TRACK **3**
Listen to the introductions. Who is speaking? Write the number of the conversations under the correct people.

B CD 1 TRACK **4**
Listen again. Write *Ms.* or *Mr.* on the line.

Conversation 1

Tom: Hi, I'm Tom Bailey.

Sharon: Hi, I'm Sharon McLean.

Tom: It's nice to meet you, _____ McLean.

Sharon: It's nice to meet you, too.

Please call me Sharon.

Tom: And please call me Tom.

Conversation 2

Norma: Hello. I'm Norma Sanchez.

André: Hi. My name is André Charles.

Norma: It's nice to meet you, _____ Charles.

André: It's nice to meet you, too.

Please call me André.

Norma: And please call me Norma.

Hello. My name is Tina Young.

Hello. I'm John Chan.

Grammar to Communicate 1

BE: AFFIRMATIVE STATEMENTS WITH *AM / IS*

Subject Pronoun	*Be*		Contractions
I	am	Tom.	I + am → I'm
It	is	nice to meet you.	It + is → It's

Possessive Adjective	Noun	*Be*	
My	name	is	Tom.

A Complete the conversation. Use the words in the box. You may use a word more than one time. Be careful! Use capital letters as needed.

I'm	is	it's	my

Rosa: Hi. ___I'm___ Rosa Vega.

Jenny: Hi. _____ name _____ Jenny Cho.

Rosa: _____ nice to meet you.

Jenny: _____ nice to meet you, too.

B Write *'m*, *'s*, or *is* on the lines. Use contractions if possible.

1. I___'m___ Ivana Polsky.

2. My name _____ Maria Ramirez.

3. I _____ Jean LeClerc.

4. It _____ nice to meet you.

5. My last name _____ White.

6. My first name _____ Claire.

See Pronunciation Activity A: page 197

C Complete the sentences. Use the verb *be*. Use contractions if possible.

1.

   My name _____ Manny Alba.

2.

   I _____ Susan Gray.

3.

   My name _____ Charles Tanner.

4.

   My first name _____ Grace. My last name _____ Wong.

TIME to TALK

CLASS. **Walk around the room. Introduce yourself to your classmates.**

Example:
A: *Hi. I'm Sonia Bermudez.*
B: *Hello. My name is Lynn Shu.*
A: *It's nice to meet you, Lynn.*
B: *It's nice to meet you, too. Excuse me. What's your name again?*
A: *Sonia.*

Look
You can say, *Excuse me. What's your name again?*

CLASS. **Now introduce one classmate to the class.**

Example:
A: *This is Lynn Shu.*
Class: *It's nice to meet you, Lynn.*

Look
Use *This is* to introduce two people to each other.

It's nice to meet you. 5

The English Alphabet

 5 **Read and listen. Then listen and repeat.**

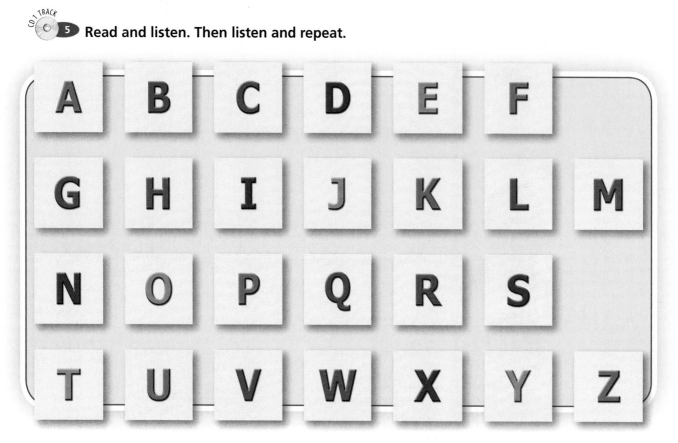

PAIRS. **Student A, say a letter. Student B, point to the letter. Take turns.**

Example:

A: *B.*
B: *Could you repeat that, please?*
A: *B.*
B: *(Points to the letter B)*
A: *Right!*

Look

You can say,
Could you repeat that, please?

PAIRS. **Practice the conversation. Use your own information.**

Example:

A: *What's your last name?*
B: *Smith.*
A: *Could you spell that, please?*
B: *S-M-I-T-H.*
A: *S-M-I-T-H?*
B: *Right.*

Look

You can say,
Could you spell that, please?

Listening

A **CD 1 TRACK 6** **Listen to a conversation. Circle the last names.**

1. Kim's last name is
    a. Rardin   **b.** Reardon   **c.** Reardin
2. Rob's last name is
    a. Conrad   **b.** Konrad   **c.** Conran

B **CD 1 TRACK 7** **Listen to two conversations. Write the names on the lines.**

Conversation 1

Steve and Rob are talking about _____.
(name)

Conversation 2

Silvia and Kim are talking about _____.
(name)

C **CD 1 TRACK 8** **Listen again. Write the missing words.**

Conversation 1

Steve: Who's that?

Rob: Her name is Kim Rardin. She's _____.

Conversation 2

Silvia: Who's that with Steve?

Kim: His _____ is Rob Konrad. He's nice.

It's nice to meet you.

Grammar to Communicate 2

PRONOUNS *HE / SHE*			
Pronoun			**Contractions**

	Pronoun			Contractions
	He		nice.	He + is ⟶ **He's**
		is		She + is ⟶ **She's**
	She		my teacher.	

Look

Use capital letters for the first word of a sentence:
He's nice.
for names:
Mr. Rob Konrad

A Complete the sentences. Use *He's* or *She's*. Write the words on the lines.

1.

   __He's__ my classmate.

2.

   That's Ms. Moreno. _____ my teacher.

3.

   _____ cute.

4.

   _____ my classmate.

5.

   That's Pete. _____ nice.

6.

   Wen Jen is my classmate. _____ nice.

See Pronunciation Activity B: page 197

POSSESSIVE ADJECTIVES: *HIS / HER*			
Possessive Adjectives	Noun		
His	name	is	Rob.
Her			Ms. Rardin.

B Write *his* or *her* on the lines. Be careful! Sometimes you will need to use a capital letter.

1. **A:** Who's that?

    B: That's my teacher. __Her__ name is Ana. She's nice.

2. **A:** Who's that?

    B: That's my classmate. _____ name is Henry. He's nice.

3. **A:** Who's that?

    B: That's my friend. _____ name is Barbara. She's nice.

4. **A:** Who's that man?

    B: _____ name is David.

    A: What's _____ last name?

    B: Hmm. I think _____ last name is Morton.

C  CD 1 TRACK 9 **Listen. Check your answers.**

PAIRS. **Practice the conversations in Exercise B.**

TIME to **TALK** **GROUPS. Student A, begin. Say your name. Student B, say Student A's name. Then say your name. Continue.**

Example:
A: *My name is Lynn.*
B: *Her name is Lynn. My name is Carlos.*
C: *Her name is Lynn. His name is Carlos. My name is Henry.*

It's nice to meet you. **9**

Reading and Writing

Reading

A   **Look at the form. Read each sentence below. Circle the correct word.**

___*X*___ Mr.   ___Ms.   ___Miss   ___Mrs.   ___Dr.

___*Oliver*___   ___*Ben*___   ___*R.*___
Last name   First name   Middle initial

1. The person is **a man / a woman**.

2. His **first / last** name is Ben.

3. His **first / last** name is Oliver.

4. His **middle name / middle initial** is R.

B   **Look at the form. Read each sentence below. Correct the mistake. Write a correct sentence.**

___Mr.   ___*X* Ms.   ___Miss   ___Mrs.   ___Dr.

___*Bonds*___   ___*Catherine*___   ___*Anne*___
Last name   First name   Middle name

1. The person is a man.   The person is a woman.

2. Her first name is Bonds.   _____

3. Her last name is Catherine.   _____

4. Her middle initial is Anne.   _____

Prewriting

Answer the questions about yourself. Write sentences.

1. What's your first name?

   _____

2. What's your last name?

   _____

3. What's your middle name?

   _____

4. What's your middle initial?

   _____

Writing

Fill out the forms with true information. Use the forms on page 10 as a model.

___Mr.   ___Ms.   ___Miss   ___Mrs.   ___Dr.

_____   _____   _____
Last name   First name   Middle initial

___Mr.   ___Ms.   ___Miss   ___Mrs.   ___Dr.

_____   _____   _____
Last name   First name   Middle name

Review

Put It in Place

A Complete the chart with *I* and *my*. Use capital letters.

I	am 'm	Sue.		name	is	Sue.

B Complete the chart with *he*, *she*, *his*, and *her*. Use capital letters.

_____	is 's	nice.	_____	name	is	John.
_____			_____			Ana.

Put It Together: Spelling

PLAYERS	2 students
MATERIALS	2 books
GOAL	To ask for and give the spelling of names
EXAMPLE	Student A: Person 1. His first name is Jamie. Student B: Could you spell that, please? Student A: J-A-M-I-E.
HOW TO PLAY	See page 215.

Student A

Give and spell the names of these people.

1. Jamie Foxx

2. Cameron Diaz

3. Hideki Matsui

4. Johnny Depp

Write Student B's names here.

5. Jennifer Lopez

6. _____

7. _____

8. _____

Student B

Write Student A's names here.

1. Jamie Foxx

2. _____

3. _____

4. _____

Give and spell the names of these people.

5. Jennifer Lopez

6. Manny Ramirez

7. Venus Williams

8. Jet Li

It's nice to meet you. 13

Vocabulary

CD 1 TRACK **10** **Read and listen. Then listen and repeat.**

1. Ireland
2. England
3. Germany
4. France
5. Spain
6. Italy
7. Somalia
8. Russia
9. India
10. China
11. Korea
12. Japan
13. Taiwan
14. Canada
15. The United States
16. Mexico
17. Peru
18. Brazil

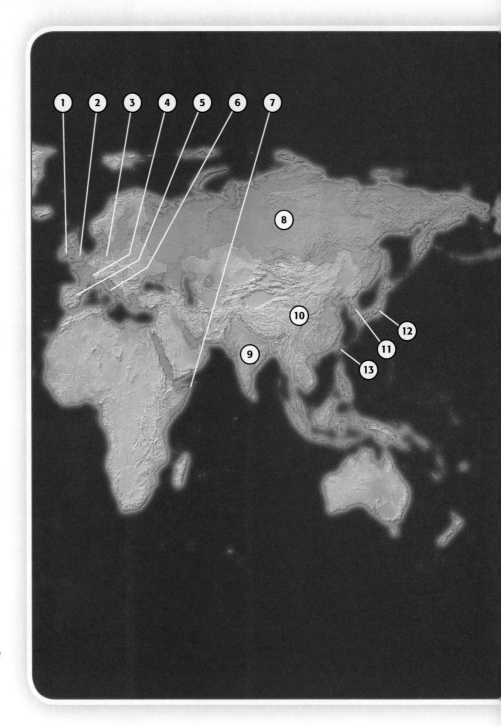

PAIRS. **Practice the conversation. Then make a new conversation. Use true information.**

Example:
A: *I'm from Mexico. And you?*
B: *I'm from Russia.*

See Pronunciation Activity A: page 198

Listening

Jim is introducing Bill to Shanti.

A 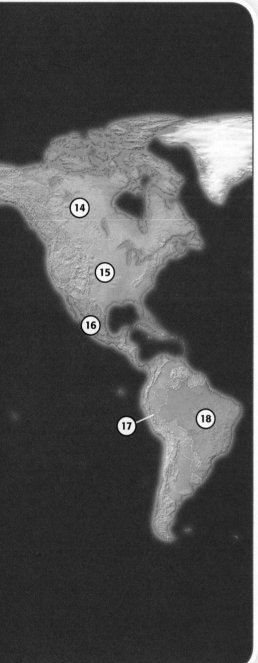 **11 Listen to the conversation. Check (✓) the countries you hear.**

❑ England   ❑ Ireland   ❑ India

B **12 Listen again. Fill in the blanks.**

Jim: Shanti, this _____ Bill. Bill, this is Shanti.

Shanti: Nice to meet you, Bill.

Bill: Nice to meet you, _____.

Jim: Shanti is _____ India.

Shanti: Well, actually, I'm not from India.

My parents are from India.

I'm from England.

Jim: You're from England? Sorry!

Shanti: That's OK.

Grammar to Communicate 1

BE: STATEMENTS

Affirmative			Negative				Contractions
Subject Pronoun	*Be*		**Subject Pronoun**	*Be*	*Not*		I + am → I'm
I	am		I	am			You + are → You're
You	are		You	are			He + is → He's
He She It	is	from Peru.	He She It	is	not	from Spain.	She + is → She's It + is → It's We + are → We're
We They	are		We They	are			They + are → They're

A **Rewrite the sentences. Use contractions.**

1. I am not from Mexico. I am from Peru. _I'm not from Mexico. I'm from Peru._

2. We are from Italy. We are not from Spain. _____

3. She is from Taiwan. She is not from the U.S. _____

4. He is not from Brazil. He is from Japan. _____

5. It is from Korea. It is not from China. _____

6. They are not from Germany. They are
   from Russia. _____

PAIRS. **Compare your answers.**

B **Fill in the blanks. Use the words in the box.**

He's   It's   She's   They're   We're   You're

1. This is Mr. Arias. ____He's____ from Spain.

2. That's Faduma and that's Hassan. _____ from Somalia.

3. This is Mrs. Ahn. _____ from Korea.

4. This is Dawn and I'm Tim. _____ from Ireland.

5. _____ nice to meet you. _____ from the U.S., right?

6. That's Mr. Strauss. _____ from Canada.

C **The sentences are not correct. Correct the mistakes. Write two sentences.**

1. Mr. Iyer is from England. (India)

   <u>Mr. Iyer is not from England. He's from India.</u>
   _____

2. I'm from Spain. (Mexico)

   _____
   _____

3. Ms. Marche is from Canada. (France)

   _____
   _____

4. Jae-Min and I are from the U.S. (Korea)

   _____
   _____

5. Helen is from Japan. (China)

   _____
   _____

6. Edward and Rose are from England. (Ireland)

   _____
   _____

TIME to TALK

PAIRS. **Student A, make a sentence about a classmate's country, but make a mistake! Student B, correct the sentence. Take turns.**

Example:
A: _Eun Jun is from Taiwan._
B: _No, she's not. She's from Korea. Valerie is from Mexico._

Report to the class.

Example:
Eun Jun is not from Taiwan. She's from Korea.

Vocabulary

 13 **Read and listen. Then listen and repeat.**

THE GROCER

International Foods

spaghetti	barbecue	tacos	fried chicken	Black Forest cake
Italy	*Korea*	*Mexico*	*the U.S.*	*Germany*
Italian	**Korean**	**Mexican**	**American**	**German**

fried rice	sushi	fish and chips	paella
China	*Japan*	*England*	*Spain*
Chinese	**Japanese**	**British**	**Spanish**

PAIRS. Practice the conversation. Then make a new conversation. Take turns.

Examples:

A: *Sushi is Italian.*

B: *No, it's not. It's Japanese. Tacos are Spanish.*

A: *No, they're not. They're Mexican.*

Listening

 14 Listen to the conversation. Check (✓) the foods you hear.

Bruce and Denise are talking about popular foods in the U.S.

❏ French fries

❏ hamburgers

❏ sandwiches

❏ pizza

❏ ice cream

 15 Listen again. Fill in the missing words.

Bruce: This is interesting! Some American foods aren't really American!

Denise: Really?

Bruce: Yes! Here. Try this. Is pizza American?

Denise: No, it isn't. It's _____.

Bruce: You're right. OK. What about sandwiches? Are they American?

Denise: Yes, they are!

Bruce: Wrong! They're not American. They're _____!

Denise: Wow!

Grammar to Communicate 2

BE: YES / NO QUESTIONS AND SHORT ANSWERS

Yes / No Questions				Short Answers						Contractions	
Be	Subject Pronoun			Subject Pronoun	Be		Subject Pronoun	Be		is + not ⟶ isn't	
Am	I			you	are.		you	are not.		are + not ➜ aren't	
Are	you	British?	Yes,	I	am.	No,	I	am not			
	we			we	are.		we	are not.			
	they			you			you				
				they			they				
Is	he she it			he she it	is.		he she it	is not.			

A Complete the sentences. Use the verb *be*.
Use contractions if possible.

Look

Do not use contractions with affirmative short answers.
Yes, I am. Yes, she is.

1. **A:** ____*Are*____ you Russian?

   B: Yes, I ___*am*___. I ___'m___ from Moscow.

2. **A:** _____ your teacher American?

   B: No, she _____. She _____ Canadian.

3. **A:** _____ Mr. and Mrs. Moon Korean?

   B: Yes, they _____. They _____ from Seoul.

4. **A:** _____ León French?

   B: No, he _____. He _____ from Spain.

5. **A:** _____ you and Masa Japanese?

   B: Yes, we _____. We _____ from Tokyo.

B  **16** Listen and check your answers.

PAIRS. Practice the conversations in Exercise A.

See Pronunciation Activity B: page 198

C Write *yes / no* questions. Use the words. Then look at the pictures.
Answer the questions.

1. Chow Yun-Fat / Canadian

   Is Chow Yun-Fat Canadian?

   No, he isn't. He's Chinese.

2. Orlando Bloom / Italian

   _____

   _____

3. Antonio Banderas and
   Penelope Cruz / Mexican

   _____

   _____

   _____

4. Salma Hayek / Russian

   _____

   _____

5. Halle Berry / French

   _____

   _____

DID YOU KNOW?

Celebrity Birthplaces

Chow Yun-Fat/China   Orlando Bloom/England

Antonio Banderas and Penelope Cruz/Spain

Salma Hayek/Mexico   Halle Berry/the U.S.

TIME to TALK

GROUPS. Talk to five classmates. Ask, *Are you from the U.S.?* Write the names
and countries on a piece of paper.

Example:
A: *Valerie, are you from the U.S.?*
B: *No, I'm not. I'm from Haiti.*

Are you from Mexico? **21**

Reading and Writing

Reading

A   **Read the article.**

Foods from Around the World

Many popular foods are from different parts of the world. For example, hot dogs are from Germany. They aren't from the United States. Salsa is from Mexico. It isn't from Spain. French fries aren't from France. They're from Belgium. Spaghetti is from China. It isn't from Italy. And tea is from China, too. It isn't from England.

B   **Answer the questions. Write two sentences.**

1. Are hot dogs from the U.S.?

   No, they aren't. They're from Germany.

2. Is salsa from Spain?

   _____

3. Are French fries from France?

   _____

4. Is spaghetti from Italy?

   _____

5. Is tea from England?

   _____

Prewriting

Look at the pictures of the dances. Write two sentences about each dance.

Ballet / France

The tango / Argentina

Flamenco / Spain

Ballet is from France.

It isn't from Spain.

_____

_____

_____

_____

Belly dancing / Turkey

Step dancing / Ireland

_____

_____

_____

_____

Writing

Write an article about dances. Use your sentences from the Prewriting questions. Use the article about food on page 22 as a model.

Many popular dances are from different parts of the world. For example,

_____

_____

_____

_____

Review

Put It in Place

Complete the chart with the verb *be*. Sometimes you will need to use capital letters.

Yes / No Questions			Short Answers			
			Affirmative		Negative	
__Am__	I		you _____.	Yes,	you _____ not.	No,
_____	you	from Russia? Russian?	I _____.		I _____ not.	
	we		we _____.		we _____ not.	
	they		you _____.		you _____ not.	
			they _____.		they _____ not.	
_____	he she it		he _____.		he _____ not.	
			she _____.		she _____ not.	
			it _____.		it _____ not.	

Put It Together: Around the World

PLAYERS	2 pairs of students
MATERIALS	1 book 1 coin (Heads = move 1 box. Tails = move 2 boxes) 2 markers (1 for each pair)
GOAL	To ask and answer questions about nationalities
EXAMPLE	Student A: Is Penelope Cruz from Mexico? Student B: No, she isn't. She's from Spain.
HOW TO PLAY	See page 215.

1 Penelope Cruz / from Mexico?

2 barbecue / British?

3 spaghetti / from France?

4 sushi / Chinese?

5 fried rice / Italian?

9 Antonio Banderas / American?

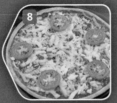
8 pizza / from Peru?

7 fish and chips / German?

6 sandwiches / from Canada?

10 tacos / Brazilian?

11 Salma Hayek / from Spain?

12 tea / from Japan?

13 hot dogs / from England?

14 Chow Yun-Fat / Korean?

FINISH

Are you from Mexico? 25

Unit 3
Who's he?

Vocabulary

CD 1 TRACK 17 **Read and listen. Then listen and repeat.**

1. grandfather
2. grandmother
3. grandparents
4. mother
5. father
6. parents
7. sister
8. brother
9. sister and brother

PAIRS. **Look at the picture. Student A, make a sentence about someone in the picture. Use *He's*, *She's*, or *They're*, for example, "He's Tania's grandfather." Student B, point to the person. Take turns.**

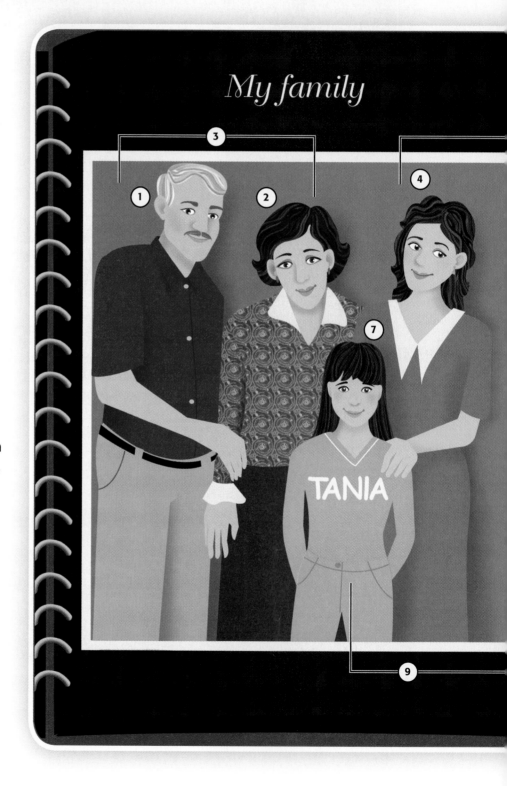

My family

Listening

Joe and Tania are talking about Tania's family.

A CD 1 TRACK 18 **Listen to the conversation. Look at the chart. Check (✓) the correct occupation for each person.**

	TEACHER	DOCTOR	ACTOR
father			
mother			

B CD 1 TRACK 19 **Listen again. Fill in the blanks.**

Joe: Is this a picture of your family?

Tania: Yes, it is. But it's an old picture.

Joe: Nice family. Who's this?

Tania: He's my _____. He's a doctor.

Joe: An actor? Cool!

Tania: No. Not an actor! A doctor!

Joe: A doctor? Oh! And this is your

_____, right?

Tania: Uh-huh. She's an English teacher.

Joe: Oh, that's great.

Grammar to Communicate 1

Look

Use *a* before words that begin with consonant sounds.
a doctor
a Canadian teacher
Use *an* before words that begin with vowel sounds.
an actor
an American student

A / AN WITH SINGULAR NOUNS

A	Noun	An	Noun
a	teacher doctor	an	actor English teacher

A Look at the pictures. Fill in the blanks with *a* or *an*.

1.

  a salesperson

2.

  ____ artist

3.

  ____ assistant

4.

  ____ dentist

5.

  ____ lawyer

6.

  ____ homemaker

7.

  ____ painter

8.
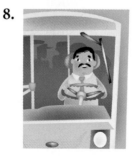
  ____ bus driver

9.

  ____ engineer

B  **20** Listen and check your answers.

C Complete each sentence with *a* or *an*.

1.
   This is my husband, Jake.

   He's __an__ artist.

2.
   This is my wife, Yvonne.

   She's _____ lawyer.

3.
   This is my girlfriend, Mona.

   She's _____ student.

4.
   This is my boyfriend, Edgar.

   He's _____ actor.

5.
   This is my friend Martha.

   She's _____ teacher.

6.
   This is my friend Steve.

   He's _____ engineer.

TIME to TALK

PAIRS. **Draw a picture (or show a photo) of your family and friends. Who is each person? What is each person's occupation? Tell your partner. Ask your teacher if you need help with occupations.**

Example:
This is my wife, Linda. She's a student.

Numbers

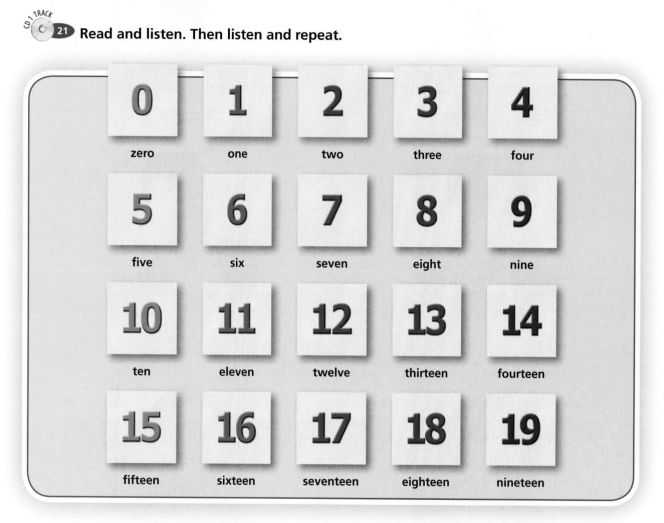

CD 1 TRACK **21** **Read and listen. Then listen and repeat.**

0 zero	1 one	2 two	3 three	4 four
5 five	6 six	7 seven	8 eight	9 nine
10 ten	11 eleven	12 twelve	13 thirteen	14 fourteen
15 fifteen	16 sixteen	17 seventeen	18 eighteen	19 nineteen

PAIRS. Student A, say a number. Student B, say the next number. Take turns.

Example:

A: *Five.*
B: *Six.*
A: *Right!*
B: *Eleven.*
A: *Twelve.*
B: *Right!*

Listening

Look

a son
a daughter } a **child**

a son and a daughter
two daughters
three sons } **children,**
or **kids** (informal)

A CD 1 TRACK 22 **Listen. Check the picture that matches the conversation.**

❑ a.

❑ b.

❑ c.

❑ d.

B CD 1 TRACK 23 **Listen again. Write the numbers on the lines.**

Mrs. Silver: Is this a picture of your family?

Mrs. Santos: Yes. This is my son, Hector.

Mrs. Silver: How old is he?

Mrs. Santos: He's _____.

Mrs. Silver: He's cute.

Mrs. Santos: Thank you! And this is my daughter, Elena.

Mrs. Silver: She's cute, too. How old is she?

Mrs. Santos: She's _____. They're great kids.

Mrs. Silver: You're very lucky!

BE: INFORMATION QUESTIONS

Wh- word	Be	Subject	Answers		Contractions
How old		she?	She's 12.		
Where	is	he?	He's in Tampa.		What + is → What's
What		his name?	His name is Hector.		Who + is → Who's
Who		she?	She's my mother.		
How old		they?	He's 9 and she's 6.		
Where	are	you from?	I'm from Mexico.		
Who		they?	They're my parents.		

A Look at the answers. Choose the correct question words. Write the words on the lines.

1. **A:** _____Where_____ are you from?
   (What / Where)

   B: Korea.

2. **A:** _____'s he?
   (What / Who)

   B: He's my son, Omar.

3. **A:** _____'s your name?
   (What / Who)

   B: Natalya Ivanova.

4. **A:** _____ is your son?
   (How old / Where)

   B: He's 16.

5. **A:** _____ are your parents?
   (Where / Who)

   B: In New York.

6. **A:** _____ is your family from?
   (Where / Who)

   B: Somalia.

7. **A:** _____ are your kids?
   (How old / Where)

   B: My son is 3. My daughter is 6.

See Pronunciation Activity B: page 199

B Write a question for each answer. Use the words. Use contractions if possible.

1. A: _Where are you from?_
      (Where / you from)
   B: We're from Los Angeles.

2. A: _____
      (What / his name)
   B: James.

3. A: _____
      (Who / they)
   B: They're my parents.

4. A: _____
      (How old / your children)
   B: One son is 9 and one son is 6.

5. A: _____
      (Where / your grandmother)
   B: She's in Colombia.

6. A: _____
      (Who / that)
   B: That's my girlfriend.

PAIRS. Look at the pictures. Look at the information under the picture. Ask and answer questions. Take turns.

Example:
A: *How old is he?*
B: *He's 11.*

age 11

Taiwan

Jenny

Somalia

Peter

India

Sonia

ages 12 and 6

Who's he?   33

Reading and Writing

Reading

  A   **Read the letter.**

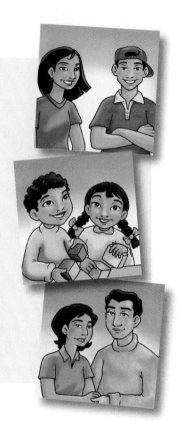

Dear Janet,

How are you?

 I'm so happy. My brother and sister are here in New Jersey with me. My brother, Tomas, is a student. He's in college. My sister, Isabel, is a housekeeper.

 Our children are great. Our son, Alex, is 6 now. He's in elementary school. Our daughter, Elizabeth, is 4. She's in pre-school.

 My husband is a taxi driver. He and I are students, too! We're in English classes at the community college.

Write soon!

Alicia

B   **Answer the questions. Write complete sentences.**

1. Where are Alicia's sister and brother?

 Her sister and brother are in New Jersey.

2. What is her sister's job?

3. Is Alicia's brother a teacher?

4. How old are her son and daughter?

5. Are they in school?

6. Are Alicia and her husband in school?

Prewriting

Think about your family and friends. Answer all the questions you can.

Parents

Are your parents alive? _____

Where are they? _____

What are their jobs? _____

Brothers and Sisters / Friends

Where are your brothers and sisters? _____

Where are your friends? _____

What are their jobs? _____

Husband / Wife

What is your husband's or wife's job? _____

Boyfriend / Girlfriend

What is your boyfriend's or girlfriend's job? _____

You

What is your job? _____

Children

How old are your children? _____

Are they in school? _____

Writing

Write a letter about your family and friends. Use the answers to the Prewriting questions. Use the letter on page 34 as a model.

_____

_____

_____

_____

_____

_____

Review

Put It in Place

A Complete the chart with *a* and *an*.

_____ painter	_____ artist
_____ lawyer	_____ assistant
_____ dentist	_____ engineer

B Complete the charts with the correct question words.

_____	is	she?	She's 12.
_____	are	your children?	They're in Santa Ana.

_____	is	his name?	Steve.
_____	's	this?	He's my friend.

Put It Together: Four in a Row

PLAYERS	2 students
MATERIALS	1 book
GOAL	To make sentences about jobs
EXAMPLE	Number 1. She's a lawyer.
HOW TO PLAY	See page 216.

Unit 4
What's your phone number?

Grammar
- Possessive Adjectives
- Possessive Nouns

Vocabulary

24 Read and listen. Then listen and repeat.

PAIRS. What's the phone number for your school? What's the e-mail address?

Phone number:

_____

E-mail address:

_____

Listening

Dario and Ruth are talking to Sandra and Greg.

A CD 1 TRACK **25** Listen to the conversation. Complete each sentence. Circle the letter of the best answer.

1. Ruth, Dario, Greg, and Sandra are _____.
   a. brothers and sisters   **b.** friends

2. Ann and Mel are from _____.
   a. the U.S.   **b.** England

B CD 1 TRACK **26** Listen again. Write the phone number.

Greg: Hi, guys!

Sandra: Hi. So what's going on?

Ruth: Oh, our friends Ann and Mel are here from England.

Dario: Yeah, why don't you come over tonight?

Greg: OK. Call us later—on our cell phone.

Ruth: Good idea. What's your number?

Greg: It's _____.

Ruth: _____. OK.

Sandra: OK. See you later.

Dario: Great.

Grammar to Communicate 1

POSSESSIVE ADJECTIVES

Subject Pronoun	Possessive Adjective	
we	our	Our friends are here from Ecuador.
you	your	What's your number?
they	their	What are their names?

A **Read the sentences. Choose the correct word. Write the word on the line.**

1. **A:** Hi. I'm Marie Dumonde. What are _____your_____ names?
   (our / your)

   B: Oscar and Agnes Leshek. Nice to meet you.

2. **A:** They're teachers. They're great.

   B: What are _____ names?
   (your / their)

3. **A:** Mr. Davis, this is _____ daughter, Lana.
   (our / your)

   B: Hi, Lana. Nice to meet you.

4. **A:** What's your address?

   B: _____ address is 245 Baker Street.
   (Their / Our)

   A: And what's _____ phone number?
   (your / our)

   B: 202-555-5398.

5. **A:** Are these your children?

   B: Yes. _____ daughter is 7. And _____ son is 4.
   (your / our)   (your / our)

6. **A:** Come to the party tonight. It's at Ellen and Ron's house.

   B: Great! What's _____ address?
   (their / your)

   A: 948 Elm Street.

B 27 **Listen and check your answers.**

PAIRS. **Practice the conversations in Exercise A.**

See Pronunciation Activity A: page 200

C Complete the sentences. Use *our*, *your*, and *their*. Be careful. Sometimes you will need to use a capital letter.

1.

My brother and I are in the U.S. ___Our___ parents are in Guatemala.

2.

You're doctors. _____ son is a doctor, too.

3.

You're in high school. _____ sister is in middle school.

4.

They're so cute. What are _____ names?

5.

This is my wife. _____ children are away at college. _____ college is in a small town.

6.

This is _____ son and his wife. This is _____ daughter. She's _____ first granddaughter.

Numbers and Addresses

 28 Read and listen. Then listen and repeat.

20 twenty	**21** twenty-one	**22** twenty-two	**23** twenty-three	**24** twenty-four	**25** twenty-five
26 twenty-six	**27** twenty-seven	**28** twenty-eight	**29** twenty-nine	**30** thirty	**40** forty
50 fifty	**60** sixty	**70** seventy	**80** eighty	**90** ninety	**100** a hundred

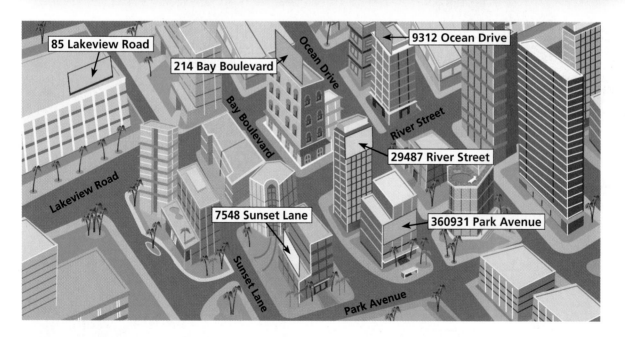

85 Lakeview Road
214 Bay Boulevard
9312 Ocean Drive
29487 River Street
7548 Sunset Lane
360931 Park Avenue

Ocean Drive
Bay Boulevard
River Street
Lakeview Road
Sunset Lane
Park Avenue

PAIRS. Student A, ask Student B for the address of each apartment for rent. Take turns.

Example:

A: *What's the address of the apartment for rent on Lakeview Road?*

B: *85 Lakeview Road.*

A: *85 Lakeview Road? Thanks.*

Listening

A CD 1 TRACK **29** **Listen to the conversations. Brad gets information. Look at the chart. Check (✓) the information he gets.**

Brad is on the phone.

	CELL PHONE NUMBER	ADDRESS
Tom's		
Alex's		

B CD 1 TRACK **30** **Listen again. Write the missing information.**

Conversation 1

Brad: Hi, Simone. It's Brad.

Simone: Hi, Brad. What's up?

Brad: Do you have Tom's cell phone number?

Simone: Sure. It's _____.

Brad: _____? OK. Thanks.

Conversation 2

Brad: Hi, Tom. It's Brad. Where are you?

Tom: Hey, Brad. I'm at Alex's apartment. Come over!

Brad: OK. What's Alex's address?

Tom: It's _____ Adams Street.

Brad: Could you repeat that, please?

Tom: _____ Adams.

Brad: Thanks. See you soon.

Grammar to Communicate 2

POSSESSIVE NOUNS

Possessive Noun	Noun
Tom's	cell phone number
Nancy's	apartment
Ms. Rush's	house
Mr. and Mrs. Watson's	e-mail address
Sharon and Marc's	home phone number

Look

We add an extra syllable when we pronounce 's after names that end in /s/, /z/, /sh/, /zh/, /ch/, /j/

Dennis ➝ Dennis's
Alex ➝ Alex's
Ms. Rush ➝ Ms. Rush's

A Read the questions. Write the answers. Use the words in parentheses.

Look

Use *at* + a specific place to answer questions with *Where*.
Tara is at Donna's house.

1. **A:** Where is Tom?

   B: He's at _____ Jack's house. _____
   (Jack / house)

2. **A:** Where is Jun?

   B: He's at _____
   (Mr. and Mrs. Park / apartment)

house

3. **A:** Where are Maggie and Ed?

   B: They're at _____
   (Bob and Rita / house)

4. **A:** Where is Gabriela?

   B: She's at _____
   (Lucy / office)

apartment

5. **A:** Where are Donna and Steve?

   B: They're at _____
   (Mr. and Mrs. Randall / apartment)

B CD 1 TRACK 31 **Listen and check your answers.**

office

See Pronunciation Activity B: page 200

C   **Write one sentence. Use possessive nouns.**

1. This is Carmen. Her address is 258 Henry Street.

   Carmen's address is 258 Henry Street.

2. This is Mr. and Mrs. Cho. Their phone number is 619-555-3298.

   _____

3. This is Janice. Her e-mail address is jan1237@coolmail.com.

   _____

4. This is Ahmet. His address is 9381 Lake Avenue.

   _____

5. This is Shanti and Vijay. Their cell phone number is 203-555-2036.

   _____

WORK ALONE. Complete the first row of the chart with your information.

GROUPS. Take turns. Ask for each other's address, ZIP code, phone number, and e-mail address. (You can use made-up information.)

NAME	ADDRESS	ZIP CODE	PHONE NUMBER	E-MAIL ADDRESS

Example:
A: *Silvia, what's your address?*
B: *193 Beach Street.*
C: *What's your ZIP code?*
B: *It's 11235.*

Report to the class. Tell one thing about someone in your group.

Example:
Silvia's address is 193 Beach Street.

Reading and Writing

Reading

A **Look at the form. Answer the questions.**

1. What's the person's name? _____

2. What's her address? _____

3. What's her phone number? _____

4. What's her e-mail address? _____

PERSONAL INFORMATION

Name	*Alicia*	*Janet*	*Cisneros*
	First	Middle	Last

Address	*4539*	*Marin Blvd.*	*2B*
	Number	Street	Apt.
	Miami	*FL*	*33125*
	City	State	ZIP Code

Phone No.	(day)	*305*	*555-1200, ext. 342*
		Area Code	
	(eve)	*305*	*555-2318*
		Area Code	
	(cell)	*305*	*555-9431*
		Area Code	

E-mail Address   *ajcisneros@coolmail.com*

B **Match the abbreviations to the words.**

_e_ **1.** Blvd.		**a.** number	
____ **2.** Apt.		**b.** Florida	
____ **3.** No.		**c.** extension	
____ **4.** eve		**d.** apartment	
____ **5.** FL		**e.** Boulevard	
____ **6.** ext.		**f.** evening	

Prewriting

Answer the questions. You can use made-up information.

1. What's your full name? _____
2. What's your street address? _____
3. What's your apartment number? _____
4. What's the abbreviation for your state? _____
5. What's your ZIP code? _____
6. What's your area code? _____
7. What's your home phone number? _____

Writing

Complete the form. You can use made-up information. Use the form on page 46 as a model.

PERSONAL INFORMATION

Name _____
First   Middle   Last

Address _____
Number   Street   Apt.

_____
City   State   ZIP Code

Phone No.   (day) _____
Area Code

(eve) _____
Area Code

(cell) _____
Area Code

E-mail Address _____

Review

Put It in Place

A Complete the chart with the correct possessive adjectives.

Subject Pronoun	Possessive Adjective
we	
you	
they	

B Complete the chart with the correct possessive nouns for the people.

Name	Possessive Noun	
Charles		cell phone number
Mr. and Mrs. Ali		apartment
Susan and Jeff		house
Talia		home phone number

Put It Together: Missing Information

PLAYERS	2 students
MATERIALS	2 books
GOAL	To ask and answer questions about addresses, telephone numbers, and e-mail addresses
EXAMPLE	Student A: What's Brad Smith's address? Student B: It's 18376 Shore Drive.
HOW TO PLAY	See page 216.

Student A's Information

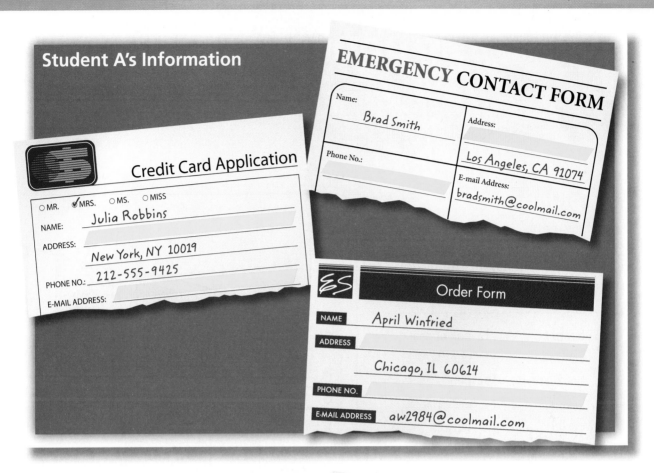

EMERGENCY CONTACT FORM

Name: Brad Smith

Address: Los Angeles, CA 91074

Phone No.:

E-mail Address: bradsmith@coolmail.com

Credit Card Application

○ MR. ◉ MRS. ○ MS. ○ MISS

NAME: Julia Robbins

ADDRESS: New York, NY 10019

PHONE NO.: 212-555-9425

E-MAIL ADDRESS:

Order Form

NAME: April Winfried

ADDRESS: Chicago, IL 60614

PHONE NO.

E-MAIL ADDRESS: aw2984@coolmail.com

Student B's Information

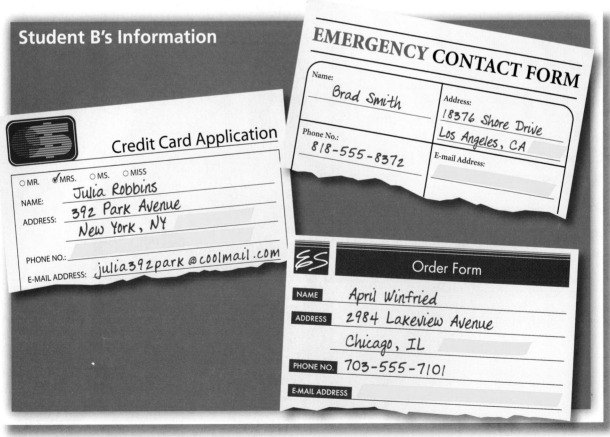

EMERGENCY CONTACT FORM

Name: Brad Smith

Address: 18376 Shore Drive
Los Angeles, CA

Phone No.: 818-555-8372

E-mail Address:

Credit Card Application

○ MR. ◉ MRS. ○ MS. ○ MISS

NAME: Julia Robbins

ADDRESS: 392 Park Avenue
New York, NY

PHONE NO.:

E-MAIL ADDRESS: julia392park@coolmail.com

Order Form

NAME: April Winfried

ADDRESS: 2984 Lakeview Avenue
Chicago, IL

PHONE NO. 703-555-7101

E-MAIL ADDRESS

Unit 5
Open your books.

Vocabulary

CD 1 TRACK 32 Read and listen. Then listen and repeat.

1. board	11. box of chalk
2. window	12. pencil
3. bookcase	13. pen
4. glasses	14. dictionary
5. eraser	15. desk
6. book	16. backpack
7. door	17. workbook
8. closet	18. on
9. chair	19. in
10. notebook	20. near

WORK ALONE. Look at the things in the picture. Are these things in your classroom? Check (✓) the things you see.

PAIRS. Compare answers.

Example:
A: *A desk, a chair, a book, a notebook, and a pen.*
B: *Yes. And a bookcase, . . .*

Listening

A 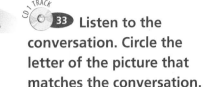 **33** **Listen to the conversation. Circle the letter of the picture that matches the conversation.**

Mike is a great teacher, but he is absent-minded. He is talking to his class.

a

b

c

B **34** **Listen again. Fill in the missing words.**

Mike: OK, class, take out your workbooks. Wait. Where's my workbook?

Pierre: It's on your _____, Mike.

Mike: Oh, yeah. Thanks, Pierre. OK, so please open your workbooks to page 10. Astrid, please come to the _____. Write sentence number 1.

Astrid: Excuse me, Mike, but where's the chalk?

Mike: The chalk? Hmm. Where's the chalk? Good question!

Javier: It's on your _____, Mike. It's over there, near the pens and pencils.

Mike: Oh, you're right, Javier. Thanks. Here's the chalk, Astrid.

Astrid: Thanks.

Mike: OK. Ready, Astrid? Wait! My glasses! Where are my glasses?

Astrid: In your hand! They're in your hand, Mike.

Open your books. 51

Grammar to Communicate 1

PLURAL OF REGULAR NOUNS

Singular		Plural		Singular			Plural		
a	book	two	books	The book			The books		
a	pen	three	pens	The pen			The pens		
an	eraser	many	erasers	The eraser	is	here.	The erasers	are	here.
a	student		students	The student			The students		

A   **Choose the correct word. Write it on the line.**

1. Where are the ___books___ ?
   (book / books)

2. Is this your _____?
   (pen / pens)

3. Andrea's _____ is on her desk.
   (dictionary / dictionaries)

4. The _____ is on the bookcase.
   (notebook / notebooks)

5. The _____ are in the box.
   (pencil / pencils)

6. Where are the _____?
   (eraser / erasers)

7. The _____ is near the door.
   (bookcase / bookcases)

Look

| a dictionary | two dictionaries |
| a box | two boxes |

For spelling rules of plural nouns, see page 213.

B   **Rewrite the sentences. Change the underlined words to the plural. Make all necessary changes.**

1. Please open the <u>box</u>.   _Please open the boxes._

2. Let's go over the <u>answer</u>.   _____

3. Where is the <u>dictionary</u>?   _____

4. Dan's <u>book</u> is on his desk.   _____

5. The closet <u>door</u> is open.   _____

6. The <u>window</u> isn't open.   _____

7. Teresa's <u>pencil</u> is in her backpack.   _____

See Pronunciation Activity A: page 201

C Complete the questions. Look at the pictures. Answer the questions. Use *on* and *in*.

1. A: Where <u>are the books?</u>

   B: <u>They're in the closet.</u>

2. A: Where _____

   B: _____

3. A: Where _____

   B: _____

4. A: Where _____

   B: _____

5. A: Where _____

   B: _____

D **35** Listen and check your answers.

PAIRS. Practice the conversations in Exercise C.

TIME to TALK

GROUPS. Each student, guess: How many books are in your group? How many pens? How many pencils? How many dictionaries? How many backpacks? Write your guesses.

Compare your answers.

Count how many books, pens, pencils, dictionaries, and backpacks you have in your group. Write the numbers. Are you right?

Vocabulary

36 Read and listen. Then listen and repeat.

PAIRS. Student A, act out an action. Student B, guess the action. Take turns.

Example:

B: *Read a sentence out loud.*
A: *Right!*

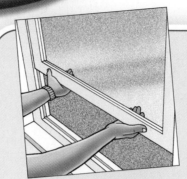

1. Open the window.

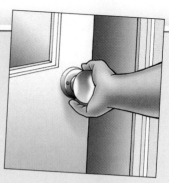

2. Close the door.

4. Write your answers.

5. Listen to the CD.

7. Look at the board.

8. Take out a piece of paper.

10. Raise your hand.

11. Use a pencil.

Listening

Mike is talking to his class.

3. Read a sentence out loud.

6. Erase the board.

9. Turn to page 23.

12. Point to the picture.

A CD 1 TRACK **37** **Listen to Mike. Look at the pictures. Number them in order.**

B CD 1 TRACK **38** **Listen again. Fill in the missing words. Use the words in the box.**

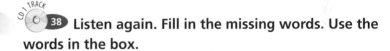

> the CD   the door   a pen   a pencil   your answers

Mike: Julio, please close _____. Thanks.

OK, everyone. Are you ready for the test? Remember.

Write _____ on the answer sheet.

Don't write on the test. Use _____.

Don't use _____. Listen to

_____. Is everyone ready? OK.

Listen carefully.

Open your books.   55

IMPERATIVES

Affirmative		Negative			Contraction
Verb		*Do + Not*	Verb		*Do + not* ⟶ **Don't**
Open Close	the door. the window. your books.	Do not	open close	the door. the window. your books.	

A Look at the pictures. Check (✓) the correct response.

1.

> **Look**
>
> Use *please* with the imperative to be polite.
> Please open the door.
> Please close the window.

- ❏ **a.** Open the closet.
- ☑ **b.** Don't open the closet.

2.

- ❏ **a.** Open the door.
- ❏ **b.** Don't open the door.

3.

- ❏ **a.** Talk to your classmates.
- ❏ **b.** Don't talk to your classmates.

4.

- ❏ **a.** Close the window.
- ❏ **b.** Don't close the window.

5.

- ❏ **a.** Look at the example.
- ❏ **b.** Don't look at the example.

See Pronunciation Activity B: page 201

B Look at the verbs on the left. Each verb goes with one pair of phrases on the right. Match the verbs on the left with the phrases on the right.

_e_ 1. turn to
____ 2. read
____ 3. take out
____ 4. listen to
____ 5. open
____ 6. write
____ 7. erase

a. sentence number 5 / a book
b. the board / the mistake
c. your name / the answers
d. the door / your book
e. page 48 / your partner
f. a pen / your workbook
g. the CD / your teacher

C Complete the sentences. Write affirmative or negative imperatives. Use the verbs in parentheses. Sometimes you will need to use a capital letter.

1. Please _____don't write_____ on the test.
                  (not write)

2. Please _____ your hand to answer.
                  (raise)

3. _____ your partner's answers, please.
      (not look at)

4. _____ and _____.
      (listen)   (repeat)

5. Please _____ out loud. _____ silently, please.
              (not read)   (read)

6. _____ your answers on the answer sheet.
      (write)

7. _____ a pen. Please _____ a pencil.
      (not use)   (use)

TIME to TALK

PAIRS. Student A, give an instruction to Student B. Student B, follow the instruction. Take turns.

Example:

Take out a piece of paper.

Reading and Writing

Reading

A Look at the pictures. Write the words under the correct picture:
Print your name, Bubble in.

_____   _____

B Imagine that you are Alex L. Smith. Follow the instructions. Complete the test application. Use the information in the box. Use today's date.

Name: Alex L. Smith   Student Identification Number: 357-08-1962
Class Number: 15113210   Teacher's name: Paloma C. Sanchez

① Last Name   First Name   Middle

② Teacher's Name

Before you take the test
1. Print your name.
2. Print your teacher's name.
3. Write your student identification number and bubble in the information below the boxes.
4. Write the test date and bubble in the information.
5. Write your class number and bubble in the information.

Right
Ⓐ ● Ⓒ Ⓓ

Wrong
⊗ Ⓑ Ⓒ Ⓓ
Ⓐ Ⓑ Ⓒ Ⓓ

③ STUDENT IDENTIFICATION

Is this your Social Security number?
Yes ⓞ   No ⓞ

④ TEST DATE

Jan Feb Mar Apr May Jun Jul Aug Sep Oct Nov Dec

⑤ CLASS NUMBER

Prewriting

Complete the information in the box. Use true information or made-up information. Use the box on page 58 as a model.

Name: _____   Student Identification Number: _____

Class Number: _____   Teacher's name: _____

Writing

Complete the test application. Use true information or made-up information. Use the application on page 58 as a model.

(1) _____
Last Name   First Name   Middle

(2) _____
Teacher's Name

Before you take the test
1. Print your name.
2. Print your teacher's name.
3. Write your student identification number and bubble in the information below the boxes.
4. Write the test date and bubble in the information.
5. Write your class number and bubble in the information.

Right
(A) ● (C) (D)

Wrong
(⊗) (B) (C) (D)
(A) (B) (Ⓒ) (D)

| (3) STUDENT IDENTIFICATION | (4) TEST DATE | (5) CLASS NUMBER |

STUDENT IDENTIFICATION

0 0 0 0 0 0 0 0 0
1 1 1 1 1 1 1 1 1
2 2 2 2 2 2 2 2 2
3 3 3 3 3 3 3 3 3
4 4 4 4 4 4 4 4 4
5 5 5 5 5 5 5 5 5
6 6 6 6 6 6 6 6 6
7 7 7 7 7 7 7 7 7
8 8 8 8 8 8 8 8 8
9 9 9 9 9 9 9 9 9

Is this your Social Security number?
Yes ◯   No ◯

TEST DATE

Jan ◯   0 0 200 0
Feb ◯   1 1 200 1
Mar ◯   2 2 200 2
Apr ◯   3 3 200 3
May ◯   4 200 4
Jun ◯   5 200 5
Jul ◯   6 200 6
Aug ◯   7 200 7
Sep ◯   8 200 8
Oct ◯   9 200 9
Nov ◯
Dec ◯

CLASS NUMBER

0 0 0 0 0 0 0 0
1 1 1 1 1 1 1 1
2 2 2 2 2 2 2 2
3 3 3 3 3 3 3 3
4 4 4 4 4 4 4 4
5 5 5 5 5 5 5 5
6 6 6 6 6 6 6 6
7 7 7 7 7 7 7 7
8 8 8 8 8 8 8 8
9 9 9 9 9 9 9 9

Review

Put It in Place

A Complete the chart with the plural.

REGULAR NOUNS		
Singular	Plural	
a desk	two	_____
a bookcase	three	_____
an exercise	many	_____

B Complete the charts with affirmative and negative imperatives. Use *read* and *write*.

Affirmative		Negative	
_____ your book.	_____ _____ your answers on the test.		

Put It Together: Slides ⚡ and Ladders 🪜

PLAYERS	2 pairs of students
MATERIALS	1 book 1 coin (Heads = move 1 box. Tails = move 2 boxes) 2 markers (1 for each pair)
GOAL	To make commands
EXAMPLE	Don't close the door. Raise your hand.
HOW TO PLAY	See page 217.

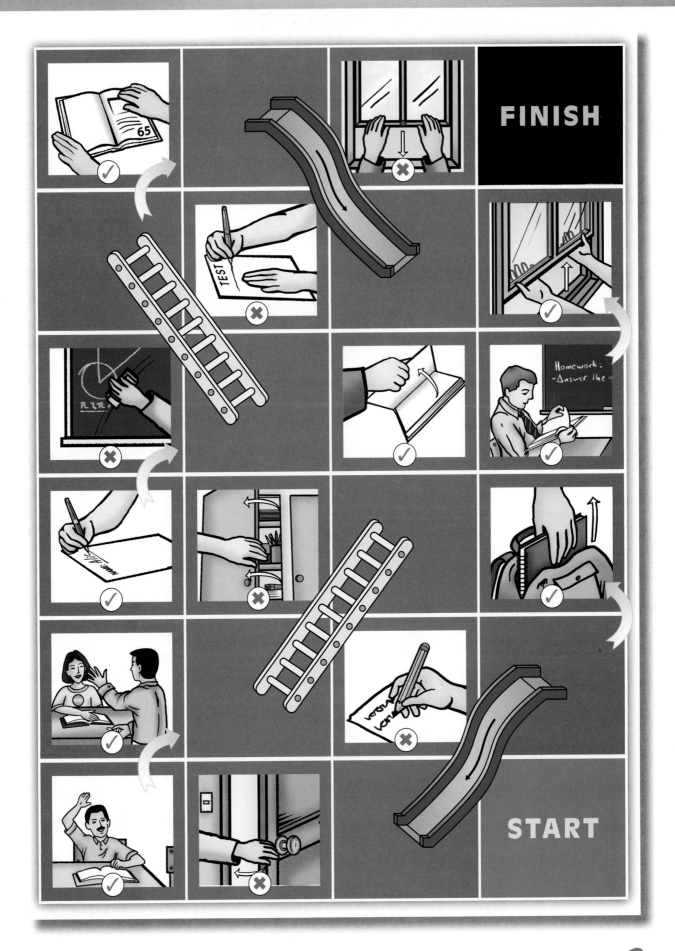

Unit 6
It's Monday morning.

Vocabulary

CD 1 TRACK **39** Read and listen. Then listen and repeat.

PAIRS. Practice the conversation. Then make a new conversation. Use true information. Take turns.

Example:
A: *What's your favorite weather?*
B: *Warm weather.*

1. hot

2. warm

4. cold

5. sunny

7. windy

8. foggy

9. rainy

See Pronunciation Activity A: page 202

Listening

A **40 Listen to the weather reports. Look at the chart. Write the temperature under the correct day.**

The weather reporter is giving a weather report.

SUNDAY	MONDAY	TUESDAY	WEDNESDAY	THURSDAY	FRIDAY	SATURDAY

B **41 Listen again. Fill in the blanks.**

Weather Report 1

And now for today's weather. It's Monday, so—of course—it's _____. Yes, it's another rainy Monday. And it's only 53°, so it's _____. Take your umbrellas and your raincoats.

Weather Report 2

Good morning, everybody! Today is Wednesday, and here's today's weather. It's _____ and it's already 85° out! Yes, it's another _____ day in New York.

Weather Report 3

Hello, everyone. It's Thursday, and here's today's weather. It's a beautiful, _____ day. It's just a little _____. The temperature is now 72°. It's a perfect day!

3. cool

6. cloudy

10. snowy

It's Monday morning. **63**

Grammar to Communicate 1

BE: INFORMATION QUESTIONS

Wh- word	Be		It + Is		Contractions
What day	is	today?		Monday.	It + is ⟶ It's
What	is	the weather today?	It's	hot.	What + is ⟶ What's
		the temperature?		85°.	

A **Look at the pictures. Complete the conversations.**

1.

A: What day is today?

B: _____

2.

A: What's the weather today?

B: _____

3.
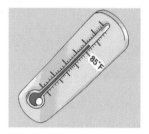

A: What's the temperature?

B: _____

4.

A: _____

B: It's Friday.

5.

A: _____

B: It's sunny.

6.
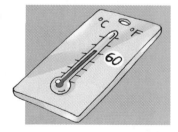

A: _____

B: It's 60°.

B   **42 Listen and check your answers.**

PAIRS. **Practice the conversations in Exercise A.**

Look at the pictures. Write three sentences for each picture.

1.

It's Sunday. It's cold and
cloudy. It's 36°.

2.

_____

_____

3.

_____

_____

4.

_____

_____

5.

_____

_____

6.

_____

_____

WORK ALONE. **You are a weather reporter. Look at the weather reports on page 63. Write a new weather report.**

Example:
Good morning. It's Tuesday in Chicago. Here's today's weather. It's windy and cold. The temperature is 42°.

PAIRS. **Take turns. Give your weather report.**

It's Monday morning.   65

Time

 43 Read the times and listen. Then listen and repeat.

1.   2.   3.   4.

 44 Read the schedule and listen. Then listen and repeat.

Look

9:00 A.M. = 9 o'clock in the morning
12:00 P.M. = 12 o'clock in the afternoon / noon
3:00 P.M. = 3 o'clock in the afternoon
6:00 P.M. = 6 o'clock in the evening
10:00 P.M. = 10 o'clock at night
12:00 A.M. = 12 o'clock in the morning / midnight

PAIRS. Practice the conversation. Then make a new conversation. Use the information in the schedule. Take turns.

Example:
A: *When is your class?*
B: *It's at 8 o'clock.*
A: *8:00 at night?*
B: *No. 8:00 in the morning.*

NEW! **Semi-Intensive English Programs**

■ Mon/Thurs Morning
9:00 A.M. – 12:00 P.M.

■ Mon/Wed Afternoon
Tues/Thurs Afternoon
3:00 – 6:00 P.M.

Listening

A **45** **Listen to three conversations. Write the number of each conversation next to the correct item.**

TIME CARD		
DAY	IN	OUT
Monday	3:00 p.m.	7:00 p.m.
Thursday	3:00 p.m.	7:00 p.m.

○

Class Schedule
English Class—M, W, F 8:45–10:30

○

ESL Placement Test

Your test has been scheduled for
Friday, March 24 at 10:00 A.M.

○

5.   5:45

6.

- Mon/Wed Evening
  Tues/Thurs Evening
  6:30 – 9:30 P.M.

- Saturday All-Day
  9:00 A.M. – 3:00 P.M.

Computer Lab Hours

Mon – Fri, 8:00 A.M. – 12:00 A.M.
Sat / Sun, 9:00 A.M. – 6:00 P.M.

B **46** **Listen again. Write the missing times.**

Conversation 1

Frank: What time is it?

Ted: It's _____ .

Frank: Oh, wow! I'm late. My English class
is at _____ .

Conversation 2

John: Where do you work, Bill?

Bill: At the bookstore.

John: What are your work hours?

Bill: _____ to _____ , Monday
and Thursday.

Conversation 3

Elena: When is your test?

Tina: On Friday.

Elena: What time?

Tina: At _____ .

Grammar to Communicate 2

BE: INFORMATION QUESTIONS

Wh- word	Be	Subject	Subject	Be		
What time	is	it? your class?	It	is	6 o'clock at 8	in the morning.
When	is	your class?	It	is	at 9	on Wednesday.
	are	your classes?	They	are	at 11:30	on Tuesday and Friday.
What	are	your work hours?	They	are	9 to 5	Monday to Friday.

A Match the questions on the left to the answers on the right.

__b__ **1.** What time is your class?

____ **2.** What time is it?

____ **3.** What are your hours?

____ **4.** When are your classes?

____ **5.** When is the test?

a. From 4:00 P.M. to 11:00 P.M.

b. It's from 6:00 to 8:30 in the evening.

c. They're on Tuesday and Thursday.

d. It's 11:15 A.M.

e. It's at 7:00.

B Read the answers. Write the questions. You can write some questions two ways.

1.

A: ___What time is it?___

B: It's 6:20.

2.

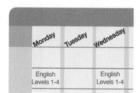

A: _____

B: They're on Monday and Wednesday.

3.

A: _____

B: Monday to Friday, 8:30 to 4:30.

4.

A: _____

B: It's at noon.

PAIRS. Compare your answers.

See Pronunciation Activity B: page 202

C Look at Roy's weekly planner. Answer the questions. Use complete sentences.

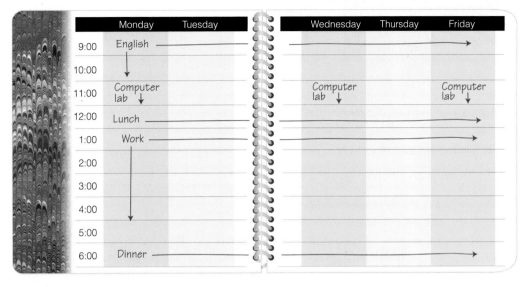

1. When are Roy's English classes?

    They're Monday to Friday, from 9:00 to 11:00.

2. When is Roy in the computer lab?

    _____

3. What time is lunch?

    _____

4. What are Roy's work hours?

    _____

5. When is dinner?

    _____

TIME to TALK

WORK ALONE. Write three questions about your classmate's schedule. Use *When*, *What*, and *What time*. Look at Exercises A, B, and C for ideas.

1. When _____?

2. What _____?

3. What time _____?

PAIRS. Ask your partner your questions. Write your partner's answers.

Report to the class. Tell the class one thing you learned about your partner.

Example:
Lee's work hours are 4:00 to 11:00 Monday to Friday.

Reading and Writing

Reading

A **Read the e-mail. Answer the questions.**

1. Who is the e-mail to? _____

2. Who is the e-mail from? _____

3. What is the e-mail about? _____

Delete	Reply	Reply All	Forward	New	Mailboxes	Get Mail	Junk

To: Mikhail@bernco.com
From: PeterZ@goodmail.com
Date: Wed., Jan. 17, 2007, 11:35 P.M.
Subject: Say hello

Hi, Mikhail.

How are you? It's 11:30 P.M. right now.

I'm really busy! I'm a cook in a restaurant. My work hours are 3:00 to 11:00 P.M. I'm in school in the morning. My English classes are from 9:00 A.M. to 12:00 P.M., Monday to Friday.

My wife is in school in the morning, too. She gets home at 1:00. Our children are in school from 8:30 to 3:00.

I don't see my family much and I'm really tired.

Peter

B **Answer the questions about Peter's schedule. Write complete sentences.**

1. What are Peter's work hours? *His work hours are 3:00 to 11:00.*

2. What days are his English classes? _____

3. When is his wife in school? _____

4. When are his children in school? _____

Prewriting

Think about your family and friends. Answer the questions you can.

You

When are you in school? _____

What are your work hours? _____

Other adults in your house

What are their work hours? _____

When are they in school? _____

Children

When are they in school? _____

Writing

Write an e-mail about the people in your household. Use the answers to the Prewriting questions. Use the e-mail on page 70 as a model.

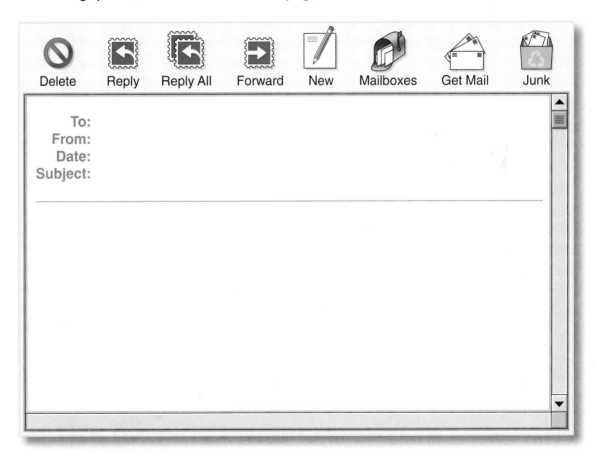

| Delete | Reply | Reply All | Forward | New | Mailboxes | Get Mail | Junk |

To:
From:
Date:
Subject:

Review

Put It in Place

A Complete the charts. Use *is*, *'s*, and *It's*.

What	day	_____	today?		Tuesday.
			the weather today?	_____	sunny.
		_____	the temperature?		75°.

B Complete the chart with *What*, *When*, *What time*, *at*, *on*, *in*, and *to*.

_____	is	it?	It	's	9:00.
_____	is	your class?	It	's	_____ Saturday.
	are	your classes?	They	're	_____ 10:45 _____ the morning.
_____	are	your work hours?	They	are	7 _____ 11 _____ night.

Put It Together: Missing Information

PLAYERS	2 students
MATERIALS	2 books
GOAL	To ask and answer about the weather, time, days, and dates.
EXAMPLE	Student A: Number 1. What day is April 20? Student B: It's Tuesday.
HOW TO PLAY	See page 217.

Student A's Information

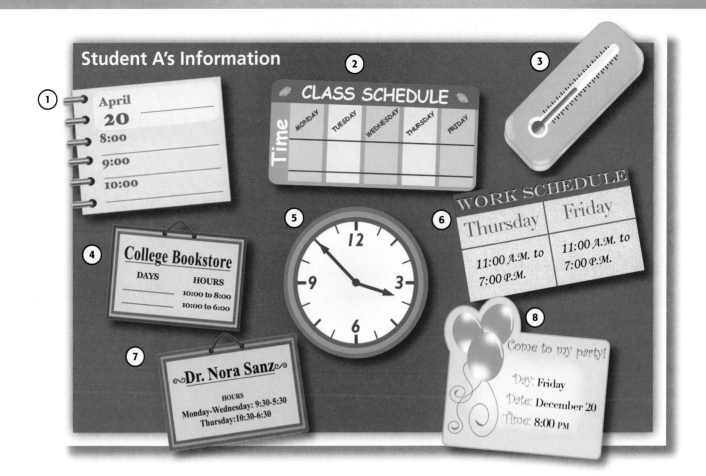

(1) April **20** 8:00 9:00 10:00

(2) CLASS SCHEDULE

Time	MONDAY	TUESDAY	WEDNESDAY	THURSDAY	FRIDAY

(3) *(thermometer)*

(4) College Bookstore

DAYS	HOURS
_____	10:00 to 8:00
	10:00 to 6:00

(5) *(clock)*

(6) WORK SCHEDULE

Thursday	Friday
11:00 A.M. to 7:00 P.M.	11:00 A.M. to 7:00 P.M.

(7) ∞Dr. Nora Sanz∞

HOURS
Monday-Wednesday: 9:30-5:30
Thursday: 10:30-6:30

(8) Come to my party!

Day: Friday
Date: December 20
Time: 8:00 PM

Student B's Information

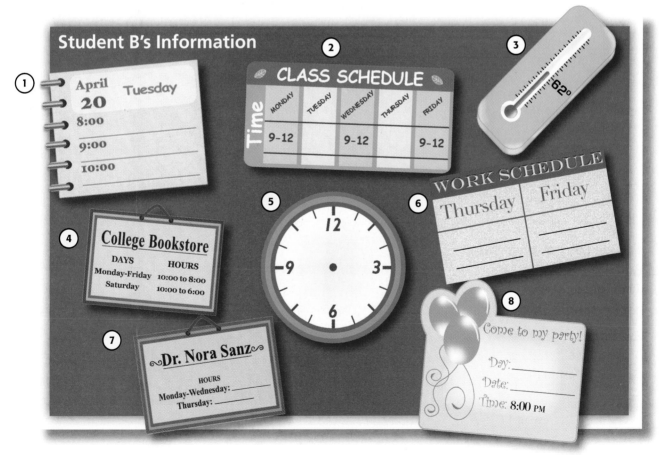

(1) April **20** Tuesday 8:00 9:00 10:00

(2) CLASS SCHEDULE

Time	MONDAY	TUESDAY	WEDNESDAY	THURSDAY	FRIDAY
	9–12		9–12		9–12

(3) 62° *(thermometer)*

(4) College Bookstore

DAYS	HOURS
Monday-Friday	10:00 to 8:00
Saturday	10:00 to 6:00

(5) *(clock)*

(6) WORK SCHEDULE

Thursday	Friday
_____	_____

(7) ∞Dr. Nora Sanz∞

HOURS
Monday-Wednesday: _____
Thursday: _____

(8) Come to my party!

Day: _____
Date: _____
Time: 8:00 PM

Unit 7
These jeans are on sale.

Grammar
- Demonstrative Adjectives: *This / That / These / Those*
- Questions with *How Much*
- Questions with *What Color*

Vocabulary

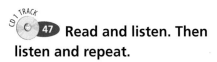 **47** **Read and listen. Then listen and repeat.**

1. jeans
2. polo shirts
3. skirts
4. blouses
5. dresses
6. jackets
7. sweaters
8. shoes
9. sneakers
10. ties
11. T-shirts
12. socks
13. coats
14. suits
15. pants
16. next to

PAIRS. **Look at the picture. Practice the conversation. Then make a new conversation. Take turns.**

Example:
A: *Where are the jeans?*
B: *They're next to the polo shirts.*

Listening

A CD 1 TRACK 48 **Listen to the conversation. Look at the shopping lists. Check (✓) the correct shopping list.**

Marcy and Lois are shopping for clothes.

☐ polo shirt
sweater

☐ T-shirt
sneakers

☐ skirt
sweater

B CD 1 TRACK 49 **Listen again. Fill in the missing words.**

Marcy: OK. What's on my list? A _____ for Joe.

Lois: Here they are.

Marcy: Oh, yeah? Great!

Lois: How about this shirt?

Marcy: Perfect. What else is on my list? A _____—for me! Where are the sweaters?

Lois: Over here. Look. These sweaters are on sale today, too. Buy one, get one free.

Marcy: Oh! That sweater is cute. And here's my size.

Lois: Hey, here's an idea. How about *you* buy one, and *I* get one free?

Buy One Get One Free

These jeans are on sale.

DEMONSTRATIVE ADJECTIVES: *THIS / THAT / THESE / THOSE*			
This / That	Singular Noun	*These / Those*	Plural Noun
this	sweater	these	sweaters
that		those	

Look

Use *this* and *these* for things near you.

Use *that* and *those* for things far away from you.

This

That

These

Those

A Write *this* or *these* on the lines. Use capital letters as needed.

1. ___These___ pants are on sale.

2. Is _____ skirt Andrea's?

3. _____ sweater is my favorite color.

4. Are _____ sneakers on sale?

B Write *that* or *those* on the lines. Use capital letters as needed.

1. Is ___that___ suit on sale?

2. Are _____ pants Rashid's?

3. _____ shirt is my size.

4. _____ shoes are nice.

See Pronunciation Activity A: page 203

C Look at the pictures. Write *this*, *that*, *these*, or *those* on the lines. Sometimes you will need to use capital letters.

1.

Is __this__ blouse on sale?

2.

_____ socks are my favorite kind.

3.

_____ jacket is nice.

4.

Are _____ jeans on sale?

5.

_____ T-shirt is a great color.

6.

_____ shirts are cool.

D **50** **Listen and check your answers.**

GROUPS. Look at your clothes. Point to your clothes and make three true statements. Tell your group.

Example:
This T-shirt is my favorite color. These jeans are old. These sneakers are new.

Vocabulary

51 **Read and listen. Then listen and repeat.**

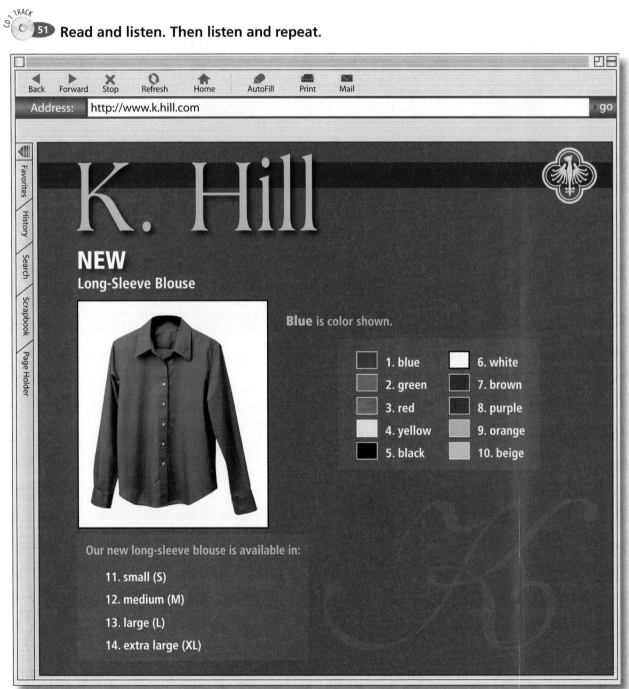

PAIRS. Look around the room. Student A, say an item of clothing. Student B, say the color.

Example:

A: *Edwina's sweater?*
B: *It's purple.*
A: *Yes!*

Listening

A father and daughter are shopping online for a gift.

A CD 1 TRACK **52** Listen to the conversation. Check (✓) the correct item.

B CD 1 TRACK **53** Listen again. Fill in the missing words. Use the words from page 78.

Daughter: Dad! It's Mom's birthday next week.

Let's go to the K. Hill Web site for her gift.

Father: Great idea. OK. What about a blouse for her new skirt?

Daughter: OK. Look. These blouses are really pretty. And they're on sale.

Father: Good. How much are they?

Daughter: They're $29.99. The regular price is $39.99.

Father: Great. She's a size _____.

Daughter: What color is her new skirt?

Father: Color? I don't know. Black . . . or _____ . . . or brown?

Daughter: I know! Let's get a _____ blouse!

Father: Perfect!

These jeans are on sale. **79**

Grammar to Communicate 2

QUESTIONS WITH *HOW MUCH*			
Wh- word	*Be*	Noun	
How much	is	the jacket?	It's $59.99.
	are	the jeans?	They're $15.99.

Look

$59.00 = We say fifty-nine dollars.
$15.99 = We say fifteen ninety-nine. (We don't say "dollars.")

A   Complete the questions. Write *How much is* or *How much are* on the lines.

1. _____How much are_____ the pants?

2. _____ the dress?

3. _____ the shoes?

4. _____ the socks?

5. _____ the T-shirt?

6. _____ the coat?

7. _____ the shirts?

8. _____ the blouse?

B   Look at the receipt. Answer the questions in Exercise A. Write complete sentences.

1. _____The pants are $18.99._____

2. _____

3. _____

4. _____

5. _____

6. _____

7. _____

8. _____

K. Hill

Shop with us online at www.k.hill.com

Pants	$ 18.99
Dress	$ 24.99
Shoes	$ 17.99
Socks	$ 2.99
T-shirt	$ 5.99
Coat	$ 79.99
Shirts	$ 24.99
Blouse	$ 15.99

C   **54** Listen and check your answers.

QUESTIONS WITH *WHAT COLOR*

Wh- word	*Be*	Noun	
What color	is	the jacket?	It's brown.
	are	the pants?	They're black.

D Look at the picture. Look at the answers. Write questions.

1. **A:** <u>What color are the sneakers?</u>

   B: They're white.

2. **A:** _____

   B: It's green.

3. **A:** _____

   B: They're red.

4. **A:** _____

   B: It's blue.

5. **A:** _____

   B: It's black.

6. **A:** _____

   B: They're blue.

7. **A:** _____

   B: It's white.

8. **A:** _____

   B: They're green.

PAIRS. Student A, cover the picture in Exercise D. Ask about the price of the sweater, the shirt, the pants, and the sneakers. Student B, answer and say if the item is expensive or inexpensive. Then switch roles. Student B, cover the picture in Exercise D. Ask about the price of the socks, the jacket, the jeans, and the blouse.

Example:
A: *How much is the sweater?*
B: *It's $34.99. It's expensive.*
A: *I agree!*
B: *How much are the socks?*

Look

Inexpensive = $
Expensive = $$$$

These jeans are on sale.

Reading and Writing

Reading

A Look at the page from the mail-order catalog. Read the sentences. They are not correct. Write a correct sentence.

Back-to-school fashions you'll love

Sweaters
Colors: orange, white, purple, red, green
Sizes: S, M, L, XL, XXL
CZ 39488   **$18.99**

Jeans
Colors: in classic blue, black, brown, beige
Sizes: waist sizes 30-48; inseam 30-34
CZ 84263   **$29.99**

Jackets
Colors: black, navy, dark green, beige
Sizes: S, M, L, XL, XXL
CZ 48572   reg $89.99
Now ONLY $69.99

NEW! Denim shirts
Colors: dark blue, light blue
Sizes: S, M, L, XL, XXL
CZ 93275   **$24.99**

1. The sweater is purple.   _The sweater is white._
2. The jeans are brown.   _____
3. The denim shirt is green.   _____
4. The jacket is blue.   _____

B Answer these questions about the clothes advertised in the catalog. Write sentences.

1. How much are the jeans?   _The jeans are $29.99._
2. How much are the denim shirts?   _____
3. How much are the sweaters?   _____
4. How much are the jackets?   _____
5. What's on sale?   _____

Prewriting

Look at the page from the mail-order catalog again. Order something from the catalog. On page 82, circle the color, size, item number, and price of the clothes you want.

Example:

Back-to-school fashions you'll love

Sweaters
Colors: orange, white, purple, red, green
Sizes: S, M, L, XL, XXL
CZ 39488 $18.99

Jeans
Colors: in classic blue, black, brown, beige

Writing

Fill in the order form.

Cool Clothing Company, Inc.

1-800-555-1234

Ship to:

Name: _____

Address: _____ Apt: #: _____

City: _____ State: _____ Zip: _____

Delivery Phone: _____

ORDER FORM

Item	Item #	Quantity	Size	Color	Price	Total Price
1 Sweater	CZ 39488	2	XL	Green	$18.99	$37.98
2						
3						
4						

These jeans are on sale.

Review

Put It in Place

Complete the charts with items of clothing from page 81.

This / That	_____	is nice.

These / Those	_____	are expensive.

How much	is	the _____?	It's $19.99.
	are	the _____?	They're $15.99.

What color	is	the _____?	It's black.
	are	the _____?	They're blue.

Put It Together: Memory Game

PLAYERS	2 students
MATERIALS	1 book
GOAL	To ask and answer about the colors and prices of clothes
EXAMPLE	Student A: What color are the pants? Student B: Beige.
HOW TO PLAY	See page 218.

$11.99
All men's polo shirts

$19.99
All men's pants

$24.65
All men's shirts

$8.99
All T-shirts

$21.99
All jeans on sale

$199.99
All 100% wool suits

$7.99
All Ties

$39.99
Shoes for men

$20.99
Sneakers for men

$4.99
Package of three socks

These jeans are on sale.

Grammar

• *There Is / There Are:* Statements

• *There Is / There Are:* Yes / No Questions and Short Answers

Vocabulary

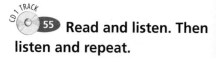 **55** **Read and listen. Then listen and repeat.**

1. children's bedroom
2. bathroom
3. parents' bedroom
4. kitchen
5. hall
6. dining room
7. living room
8. carpeting
9. blinds
10. air-conditioning

PAIRS. **Look at the picture. Ask and answer these questions. Take turns.**

Where is Mrs. Garcia?
Where is Mr. Garcia?
Where is their son?
Where is their daughter?
Where is the cat?

Example:
A: *Where is Mrs. Garcia?*
B: *She's in the dining room.*

Listening

A **56** Listen to the conversation. Check (✓) the correct apartment.

Mr. and Mrs. Garcia are looking for a new apartment.

❏ a.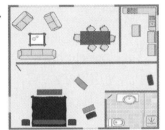

❏ b.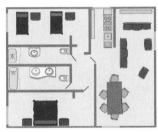

❏ c.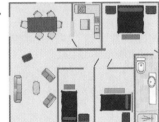

❏ d.

B **57** Listen again. Fill in the missing words.

Mrs. Garcia: Honey, listen. Here's a nice apartment.

Mr. Garcia: Oh, yeah? What's it like?

Mrs. Garcia: Well, there's a modern _____.

Mr. Garcia: Good.

Mrs. Garcia: And there's a small dining room, a sunny living room, and two _____.

Mr. Garcia: Uh-huh. How many bedrooms?

Mrs. Garcia: That's the best part. There are three bedrooms. And there are a lot of _____.

Mr. Garcia: You're right. It's great.

Mrs. Garcia: But it's not perfect. There's carpeting, but there are no _____.

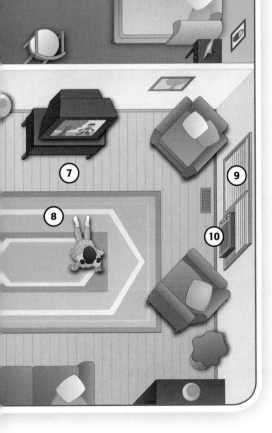

There's a sunny kitchen.   87

Grammar to Communicate 1

THERE IS / THERE ARE: STATEMENTS

There	Is / Are		Noun	Contraction
There	is	a	kitchen. living room. dining room.	There + is ⟶ There's
		no		
There	are	two a lot of	bathrooms. bedrooms. blinds.	
		no		

A Complete the sentences in the e-mail. Write *'s* or *are* on the lines.

Subject: Jessica and Adam's new apartment

Jessica and Adam's new apartment is really nice. There __'s__ one bedroom and
                                                        1.
there _____ two big closets in the bedroom. There _____ a large, sunny
              2.   **3.**
living room and there _____ carpeting. There _____ a small bathroom.
                            4.   **5.**
There _____ no dining room, but there _____ a big eat-in kitchen. There
          6.   **7.**
_____ no windows in the kitchen, so it's dark.
      8.

B Look at the notes about the apartment. Then read the sentences. Each sentence has a mistake. Correct the mistakes in each sentence.

Baldwin Road apartment

✓ bedrooms—3 large   ✓ bathrooms—two
✗ dining room   ✓ living room—sunny
✓ kitchen—small   ✗ closets

1. There is one large bedroom.   <u>There are three large bedrooms.</u>

2. There is a small dining room.   _____

3. There is no kitchen.   _____

4. There is a bathroom.   _____

5. There is no living room.   _____

6. There are a lot of closets.   _____

See Pronunciation Activity A: page 204

C Complete the conversation. Write *there's* or *there are* on the lines. Sometimes you will need to use capital letters.

Realtor: This apartment is great.

Customer: Really? What's it like?

Realtor: _____ a sunny kitchen.

Customer: That's good.

Realtor: And _____ a nice living room.

Customer: Uh-huh.

Realtor: _____ two bedrooms. One bedroom is big and one bedroom is small.

Customer: That's OK. What about a dining room?

Realtor: _____ no dining room. The kitchen is an eat-in kitchen.

Customer: Oh. What about closets?

Realtor: _____ a closet in the big bedroom, and _____ two closets in the hall.

Customer: Oh, good. And the bathroom?

Realtor: _____ a big bathroom.

D CD 1 TRACK **58** Listen and check your answers.

PAIRS. Practice the conversation in Exercise C.

TIME to TALK

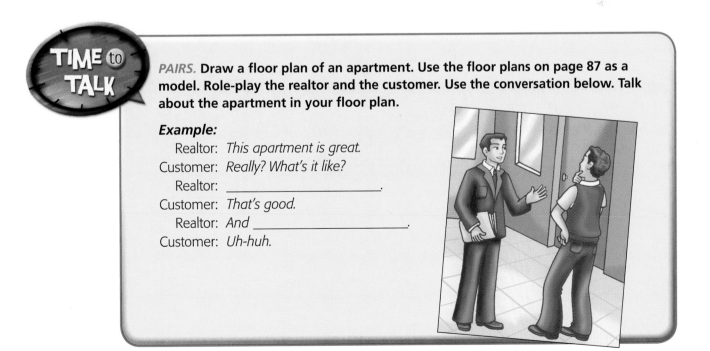

PAIRS. Draw a floor plan of an apartment. Use the floor plans on page 87 as a model. Role-play the realtor and the customer. Use the conversation below. Talk about the apartment in your floor plan.

Example:

Realtor: *This apartment is great.*

Customer: *Really? What's it like?*

Realtor: _____.

Customer: *That's good.*

Realtor: *And* _____.

Customer: *Uh-huh.*

There's a sunny kitchen.

Vocabulary and Listening

Vocabulary

CD 1 TRACK **59 Read and listen. Then listen and repeat.**

1. freezer
2. refrigerator
3. curtains
4. cabinets
5. dishwasher
6. sink
7. counter
8. microwave
9. stove
10. dryer
11. washing machine
12. chairs
13. table
14. over
15. on
16. under
17. in

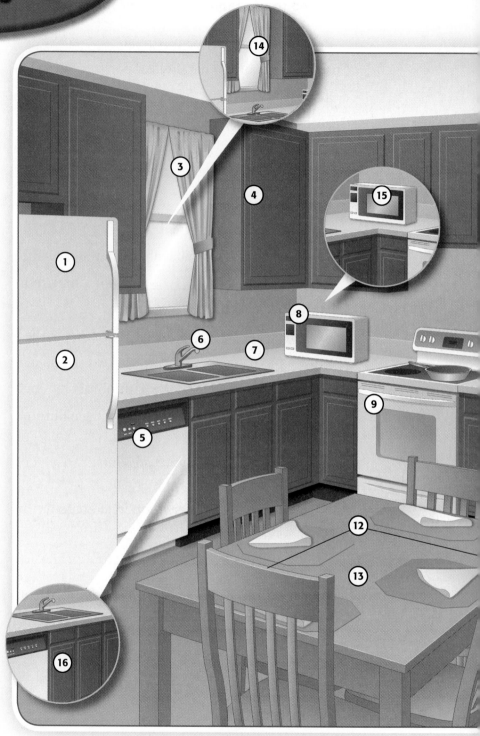

PAIRS. Look at the picture. Describe the things in the kitchen. Use *in*, *on*, *over*, *under*, and *next to*. Take turns.

Example:

A: *There's a washing machine and dryer in the closet.*

B: *There's a microwave on the counter.*

See Pronunciation Activity B: page 204

Listening

Mrs. Garcia is on the phone with the realtor.

A CD 1 TRACK 60 **Listen to the conversation. Check (✓) the things you hear.**

❑ blinds	❑ cabinets	❑ curtains
❑ a dishwasher	❑ a freezer	❑ a microwave
❑ a refrigerator	❑ a sink	❑ a stove

B CD 1 TRACK 61 **Listen again. Fill in the missing words.**

Realtor: There's a great three-bedroom apartment

for rent on Adams Street.

Mrs. Garcia: Really? What's the kitchen like?

Realtor: Oh, it's big. There's a window over the

_____, so it's nice and sunny.

Mrs. Garcia: Wonderful! Is there a dishwasher?

Realtor: Yes, there is. And there's a _____.

Mrs. Garcia: That's good. Are there any blinds on the

window?

Realtor: No, there aren't. There are _____.

There's a sunny kitchen. **91**

Grammar to Communicate 2

THERE IS / THERE ARE: YES / NO QUESTIONS AND SHORT ANSWERS

Is / Are	There	A / Any	Subject	Short Answers		
Is	there	a	dishwasher?	Yes,	there	is.
				No,		isn't.
Are	there	any	cabinets?	Yes,	there	are.
				No,		aren't.

A Write the questions. Put the words in the correct order. Use capital letters as needed.

1. _Are there any blinds on the windows?_
   (blinds / there / any / on the windows / are)

2. _____
   (there / in the kitchen / is / a / washing machine and dryer)

3. _____
   (a / is / over the stove / microwave / there)

4. _____
   (any / are / in the apartment / there / closets)

5. _____
   (are / windows / any / there / in the bathroom)

B Complete the questions with *a* or *any*. Then look at the picture. Write short answers.

1. Is there ___a___ big refrigerator?

   _No, there isn't._____

2. Are there _____ chairs?

   _____

3. Is there _____ window over the sink?

   _____

4. Are there _____ blinds on the window?

   _____

5. Is there _____ cabinet over the refrigerator?

   _____

C Write questions with *Is there* or *Are there*. Use the words in the box. Then look at the picture in Exercise B. Write short answers to the questions.

1. curtains on the window	3. windows in the kitchen	5. a table in the kitchen
2. a microwave over the stove	4. a dishwasher	6. cabinets under the counters

1. _Are there any curtains on the window?_   _Yes, there are._

2. _____   _____

3. _____   _____

4. _____   _____

5. _____   _____

6. _____   _____

WORK ALONE. Write six questions about an apartment. Begin three questions with *Is there* and three questions with *Are there*.

QUESTION	YOUR PARTNER'S ANSWERS
Is there a window in your kitchen?	
Is there	
Is there	
Are there	
Are there	
Are there	

PAIRS. Ask each other the questions. Give true answers. When the answer is *yes*, give short and long answers. Write your partner's answers.

Example:
A: *Is there a window in your kitchen?*
B: *Yes, there is. There's a window over the sink.*

Report to the class.

Example:
There's a window over the sink in Federico's kitchen.

Reading and Writing

Reading

A   Look at the ad. Match the abbreviations to the words.

> **RIVERDALE AREA** Large 2 BR,
> new BTH and EIK. Sunny LR. W/D.
> Pkg. Call Mark Ellis 818-555-3200

_d_ **1.** BR   **a.** washer and dryer

____ **2.** BTH   **b.** living room

____ **3.** EIK   **c.** parking

____ **4.** LR   **d.** bedroom

____ **5.** W/D   **e.** eat-in kitchen

____ **6.** Pkg   **f.** bathroom

B   Answer the questions about the apartment in the ad. Write sentences. Write *I don't know* if the answer is not in the ad.

1. Are there two bathrooms in the apartment?

   _No, there aren't._____

2. Is there parking?

_____

3. Is there a dining room?

_____

4. Are there three bedrooms?

_____

5. Is there a washing machine in the apartment?

_____

6. Is there a living room?

_____

Prewriting

A   Write an ad for your perfect apartment. Look at the ad on page 94 for ideas.

B   Answer questions about your perfect apartment. Write sentences.

1. Is your perfect apartment nice?   _____
2. Is it sunny?   _____
3. Are there any bedrooms?   _____
4. Are they large?   _____
5. Are there any closets in the bedrooms?   _____
6. Is the living room large?   _____
7. Is there a dining room?   _____
8. Is there an eat-in kitchen?   _____
9. Is the kitchen large?   _____
10. Are there any windows in the kitchen?   _____

Writing

Write an e-mail about your perfect apartment. Use the e-mail on page 88 as a model. Use your sentences in Exercise B. Begin, *My perfect apartment is really nice. There …*

Put It in Place

Complete the chart with *is*, *'s*, *are*, *isn't*, and *aren't*. Sometimes you will need to use a capital letter.

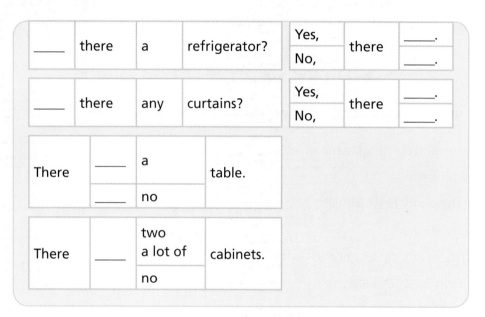

_____	there	a	refrigerator?

Yes,	there	_____.
No,		_____.

_____	there	any	curtains?

Yes,	there	_____.
No,		_____.

There	_____	a	table.
	_____	no	

There	_____	two / a lot of	cabinets.
		no	

Put It Together: Same or Different?

PLAYERS	2 students
MATERIALS	2 books
GOAL	To ask and answer about things in a kitchen
EXAMPLE	Student A: Is there a dishwasher? Student B: Yes, there's a dishwasher.
HOW TO PLAY	See page 218.

Kitchen A

Kitchen B

There's a sunny kitchen.

I want a turkey sandwich.

Grammar
- Simple Present: Affirmative Statements with *Want*, *Like*, *Need*
- Simple Present: Negative Statements with *Want*, *Like*, *Need*

Vocabulary

CD 2 TRACK 2 **Read and listen. Then listen and repeat.**

PAIRS. **Look at the list of sandwiches. What other sandwiches do you know? Make a list.**

Example:

an egg salad sandwich

Look

knife   fork   spoon

Cafe Menu

Sandwiches

1. Tuna Salad
2. Grilled Chicken
3. Turkey
4. Swiss Cheese

Soup

5. Tomato Soup

Salad

6. Mixed Green Salad

Desserts

7. Apple Pie
8. Chocolate Cake

Listening

A mother and her five-year-old son are in a coffee shop.

A CD 2 TRACK 3 Listen to the conversation. Look at the pictures. Check (✓) the foods the mother and son want.

B CD 2 TRACK 4 Listen again. Fill in the blanks with the missing words.

Conversation Part 1

Waiter: Are you ready to order?

Mom: Yes, we are. Just sandwiches today, please. I want a grilled _____ sandwich. And my son wants a _____ salad sandwich.

Waiter: Very good.

Conversation Part 2, later

Waiter: Anything for dessert?

Mom: Yes! For dessert, my son wants chocolate _____.

Joey: I like chocolate!

Waiter: Excellent!

Mom: Oh, and we both need _____.

Waiter: Certainly. That's one chocolate cake and two forks.

I want a turkey sandwich. 99

Grammar to Communicate 1

SIMPLE PRESENT: AFFIRMATIVE STATEMENTS WITH *WANT, LIKE, NEED*					
Subject	**Verb**		**Subject**	**Verb + -s**	
I You We They Mr. and Mrs. Ott	want like need	soup.	He She Mike	wants likes needs	soup.

> **Look**
>
> When the subject is *he*, *she*, or *it*, the verb always ends in *-s*.
> Taylor wants soup.
> Miss Katz likes cake.
> Her son needs a fork.

A **Complete the sentences. Choose the correct word. Write it on the line.**

1. Stacy ___wants___ a hamburger and French fries.
   (want / wants)

2. Mr. and Mrs. Ahn _____ grilled chicken
   (want / wants)

   sandwiches.

3. Michel _____ apple pie.
   (like / likes)

4. Olivia and her daughter _____ spoons.
   (need / needs)

5. My brother and I _____ chocolate ice cream.
   (like / likes)

6. Alfredo _____ a knife.
   (need / needs)

B **Complete the sentences. Use the correct form of the verbs in parentheses.**

1. My kids (like) ___like___ hamburgers.

2. Matthew and Erin (need) _____ forks.

3. My father (like) _____ Italian food.

4. Jack (want) _____ cake for dessert.

5. Ellen (need) _____ chocolate.

6. Kayla and I (want) _____ grilled chicken sandwiches.

7. Dr. Gordon (want) _____ a tuna salad sandwich.

See Pronunciation Activity A: page 205

C Complete the sentences. Use the correct form of the verb *like* or *want*.

1. Natasha likes hot dogs, but her brothers ___like___ hamburgers.

2. I want a tuna sandwich, but my husband _____ a turkey sandwich.

3. Pedro and Rosa like salads, but their children _____ pizza.

4. Hak-won likes egg salad, but his sisters _____ tuna salad.

5. Richard wants soup, but Marie _____ a salad.

6. Ms. Wong likes turkey, but her parents _____ chicken.

7. Karen and Joan want apple pie, but their boyfriends _____ chocolate cake.

8. Tom and I like French food, but our daughter _____ Italian food.

D Write a new sentence like the sentences in Exercise C. Use the verb *like*. Use true information.

_____, but _____.

PAIRS. **Student A, you are a waiter. Student B, you are a customer in a coffee shop. Use the menu. Change roles.**

Example:
Waiter: *Are you ready to order?*
Customer: *Yes. I want a salad, spaghetti, and ice cream.*
Waiter: *OK. You want a salad, spaghetti, and ice cream.*

Report to the class.

Example:
My customer wants a salad, spaghetti, and ice cream.

Soups, Salads, and Sides

Vegetable soup
Chicken soup
Garden salad
French fries

House Specials

Hamburger
Hot dog
Spaghetti
Pizza

Sandwiches

Egg salad
Tuna salad
Turkey
Grilled chicken

Desserts

Ice cream
Chocolate cake
Apple pie
Apple pie with ice cream

I want a turkey sandwich.

Vocabulary and Listening

Vocabulary

CD 2 TRACK 5 **Read and listen. Then listen and repeat.**

PAIRS. Say what you like to drink with each food in the box. Use the drinks in the pictures.

apple pie
cheese
chocolate cake
hamburgers
hot dogs
pizza
sandwiches

Example:
A: *I like coffee with apple pie.*
B: *Me, too.* OR *Not me! I like tea with apple pie.*

1. coffee

2. tea

4. milk

5. water

7. juice

8. iced tea

10. salt
11. pepper

12. glass

13. napkin

Listening

Left column images

3. hot chocolate

6. soda

9. sugar

Check
442900
coffee $1.00

14. check

A CD 2 TRACK 6 **Listen to the conversation. Look at the pictures. Number the pictures in the correct order.**

Mr. and Mrs. Brock are having lunch. There are some problems.

_____ _____ _____

B CD 2 TRACK 7 **Listen again. Write the missing words.**

Conversation Part 1

Waiter: Here you are, ma'am. Here's the salt.

Mrs. Brock: I don't need salt. I need _____!

Waiter: Oh, sorry.

Conversation Part 2, a few minutes later

Mr. Brock: Excuse me, waiter?

Waiter: Yes, sir?

Mr. Brock: My wife doesn't like her _____.
It's cold.

Waiter: Oh, sorry.

Conversation Part 3, a few minutes later

Waiter: More coffee, folks?

Mrs. Brock: We don't want more coffee. We want more _____.

Waiter: Oh, sorry.

Grammar to Communicate 2

SIMPLE PRESENT: NEGATIVE STATEMENTS WITH *WANT*, *LIKE*, *NEED*

Subject	Do / Does	Not	Verb		Contractions	
I You We They	do	not	want like need	coffee. milk. salt.	Do + not ➝ **Don't** Does + not ➝ **Doesn't**	
He She Chris	does					

A Complete the sentences. Write *don't* or *doesn't* on the lines.

1. I ____*don't*____ like hot chocolate.

2. The customer _____ want more coffee.

3. You _____ need a fork and knife for pizza.

4. Gabriela _____ like soda. She likes water.

5. We _____ want orange juice this morning.

6. My parents _____ need sugar for their tea.

7. Jim's girlfriend _____ like iced tea. She likes iced coffee.

8. The baby _____ need a glass.

> ### Look
> **Contractions**
> Use contractions in speaking and informal writing.
> *I don't want coffee.*
> *He doesn't want coffee.*

B The sentences are not true. Write true sentences.

1. Claude wants coffee.   _Claude doesn't want coffee._

2. Luis needs salt for his soup.   _____

3. The customers want the check.   _____

4. I like ice cream with apple pie. _____

5. Maya's children want iced tea.   _____

6. Han Fu needs a new napkin.   _____

7. Daria wants a glass of water.   _____

8. My boyfriend and I like soda.   _____

                    See Pronunciation Activity B: page 205

Look at the pictures. Write a sentence with *don't* or *doesn't*.

1.  Trey and Tania like milk.

   They don't like coffee.

2. 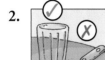 Alberto needs a glass.

   _____

3. Wen-Jen wants sugar for her iced tea.

   _____

4. Renee and Robert need spoons.

   _____

5. Fatima and Halima like apple juice.

   _____

6. Beth wants water.

   _____

TIME to TALK

WORK ALONE. Answer these questions.

Do you like coffee? ❏ Yes ❏ No

If *yes*, how do you like your coffee? ❏ Black? ❏ With milk, no sugar?
  ❏ With milk and sugar?

Do you like tea? ❏ Yes ❏ No

If *yes*, how do you like your tea? ❏ Black? ❏ With milk, no sugar?
  ❏ With milk and sugar?

**GROUPS. How do you like your coffee and tea? Tell your group.
Make three statements.**

Example:
A: *I don't like black coffee. I like coffee with milk. I like tea with milk and sugar.*

I want a turkey sandwich.

Reading and Writing

Reading

  A **Read the letter to Dr. K. What's the problem?**

> Dear Dr. K:
>
>   Our son, Bobby, is 7 years old. He is a good boy, but he is a "problem eater."
> He only likes pizza, hot dogs, and hamburgers. He doesn't want green salads or
> green vegetables, just potatoes—French fries, potato salad, or potato chips. He
> doesn't always finish his dinner, but he always wants dessert—ice cream, pie,
> and cake. When he is at other people's houses, he drinks a lot of soda. Help!
>
> Sincerely,
>
> Worried Parents

B **What are Bobby's ten favorite foods and drinks? Make a list.**

1. *pizza*
2.
3.
4.
5.
6.
7.
8.
9.
10.

PAIRS. **Discuss. Why are Bobby's parents worried?**

Writing

Bobby's five-year-old sister, Connie, is also a "problem eater." Rewrite the letter on page 106. Write about the two children.

Dear Dr. K:

Our son, Bobby, is seven years old. Our daughter, Connie, is five years old. They are good children, but _____

_____

_____

_____

_____

_____

_____

_____

_____

_____

_____

_____

_____

_____

Sincerely,

Worried Parents

Review

Put It in Place

Complete the chart with the correct form of the verb *want*.

Affirmative			Negative			
I You We They	_____	coffee.	I You We They	_____	not n't	_____	milk.
He She	_____		He She	_____			

Put It Together: Slides and Ladders

PLAYERS	2 pairs of students
MATERIALS	1 book 1 coin (Heads = move 1 box. Tails = move 2 boxes) 2 markers (1 for each pair)
GOAL	To say what people want, need, or like
EXAMPLE	Mr. Chang doesn't want iced tea.
HOW TO PLAY	See page 219.

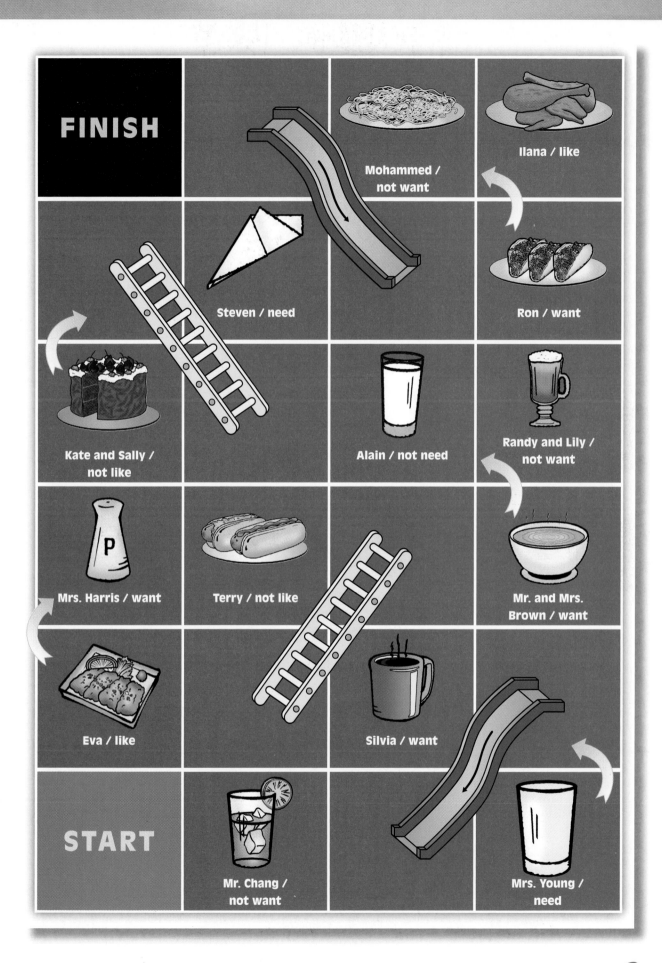

FINISH

Mohammed / not want

Ilana / like

Steven / need

Ron / want

Kate and Sally / not like

Alain / not need

Randy and Lily / not want

Mrs. Harris / want

Terry / not like

Mr. and Mrs. Brown / want

Eva / like

Silvia / want

START

Mr. Chang / not want

Mrs. Young / need

Grammar

● Simple Present:
Statements with *Have*

● Simple Present: *Yes / No*
Questions with *Have*,
Feel, Need, Want

Vocabulary

CD 2 TRACK 8 Read and listen. Then
listen and repeat.

PAIRS. Student A, act out
one of the problems in the
pictures. Student B, guess the
problem. Take turns.

Example:

B: *A cough!*
A: *Right!*

1. a cough

2. a cold

4. a fever

5. a headache

7. a sore throat

8. a stomachache

9. a backache

See Pronunciation Activity A: page 206

Listening

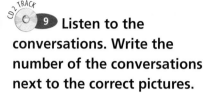 **A** **9** **Listen to the conversations. Write the number of the conversations next to the correct pictures.**

The child is in a doctor's office.

3. the flu

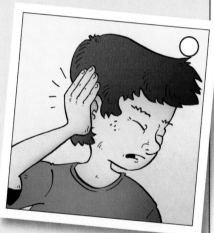

6. an earache

10. a pain

B **10** **Listen again. Fill in the blanks with the missing words.**

Conversation 1

Doctor: Hello, Ms. Curtis. Hi, Ray. How are you today?

Ray: I'm sick. I have a _____.

Doctor: OK. Let's see. Open your mouth and say "Ah."

Ray: Ah.

Doctor: Hmm.

Mother: What is it, Doctor Baum?

Doctor: He's right. His throat is very red.

Conversation 2

Doctor: Hello, Mrs. Silver. Hi, Max.

Max: Hello, Doctor Baum.

Doctor: What's the matter?

Mother: He has an _____.

Doctor: OK. Let's look. This ear?

Max: No. This ear.

Do you have a fever?

Grammar to Communicate 1

SIMPLE PRESENT: STATEMENTS WITH *HAVE*

Subject	Have / Has		Subject	Do / Does	Not	Have	
I You We They	have	the flu.	I You We They	do	not	have	the flu.
He / She	has		He / She	does			

A Complete the sentences. Choose the correct form of the verb.

1. Roger _____ has _____ a terrible cough.

(has / have)

2. Mr. Vega's son _____ a sore throat.

(doesn't have / don't have)

3. I _____ a backache today!

(doesn't have / don't have)

4. My sister _____ a bad cold.

(has / have)

5. The boys _____ earaches. They _____ colds.

(has / have)   (doesn't have / don't have)

> ### Look
> The verb *have* is irregular. For *he* and *she*, use *has*.

B Look at the pictures. Complete the conversations.

1.

   Doctor: What's the matter?

   Patient: I _have the flu._

2.

   Doctor: How is Andy today?

   Mother: He _____

3.

   Doctor: What's the matter?

   Patient: I _____

4.

   Doctor: How are May and Jen today?

   Father: They _____

C  **11** Listen and check your answers.

D Read A's sentences. Look at the names and problems below. Correct the mistake. Write two sentences.

PATIENT	PROBLEM
Jean Goulet	a headache
Kareem Al-Mansur	the flu
Nilda Sanchez	a stomachache
June Park	a headache
MaryAnn Rizzo	an earache
Berto Arias	a cold

1. **A:** Berto has a cough.

    B: _He doesn't have a cough. He has a cold._

2. **A:** MaryAnn has a sore throat.

    B: _____

3. **A:** June and Jean have backaches.

    B: _____

4. **A:** Kareem has a headache.

    B: _____

5. **A:** Nilda has a fever.

    B: _____

TIME to TALK

PAIRS. Role-play. Student B has a problem. Student A, ask, *Are you OK?* Student B, answer. Use the words from pages 110 and 111. Student A, give advice.

Example:
A: *Are you OK?*
B: *No, I have a headache.*
A: *That's too bad. You need aspirin.*

Report to the class.

Example:
Bonita has a headache. She needs aspirin.

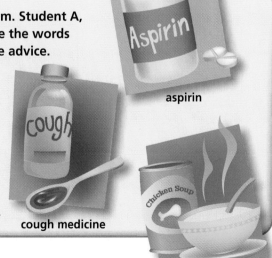

aspirin

cough medicine

chicken soup

Vocabulary

12 Read and listen. Then listen and repeat.

PAIRS. Practice the conversation. Then make a new conversation. Act it out!

Example:
A: *What's the matter?*
B: *I'm dizzy.*

1. tired

2. sick

4. hot

5. cold

7. nauseous

8. hungry

Listening

3. better

6. dizzy

Two co-workers, Gail and Eli, are talking.

A CD 2 TRACK **13** **Listen to the conversation. Circle all the problems.**

Gail has   **a.** the flu   **b.** a cough   **c.** a fever

She's   **a.** cold   **b.** hot   **c.** thirsty

B CD 2 TRACK **14** **Listen again. Fill in the blanks with the missing words.**

Eli: Hi, Gail. Are you OK?

Gail: No. I feel _____.

Eli: Oh. Why? What's wrong?

Gail: I have the flu.

Eli: Oh, no! Do you have a fever?

Gail: Yes, I do. I feel very _____.

Eli: Go home!

9. thirsty

Do you have a fever?

Grammar to Communicate 2

Do / Does	Subject	Verb		Subject	Do / Does		Subject	Don't / Doesn't
			SHORT ANSWERS					
Do	I you we they	have a fever? feel hot? need aspirin?	Yes,	you I we they	do.	No,	you I we they	don't.
Does	he she Tim	want water?		he she	does.		he she	doesn't.

A Complete the questions. Write *do* or *does* on the lines.

1. _____ you have a fever?

2. _____ Ben want chicken soup?

3. _____ Ana's children need aspirin?

4. _____ Petra feel OK?

5. _____ your friends want tea?

B Complete the questions and answers. Use *do*, *does*, *don't*, and *doesn't*.

1. **A:** ____Do____ you have a sore throat?

   B: No, I _____. I have a cough.

2. **A:** _____ Danny feel cold?

   B: Yes, he _____. He needs a sweater.

3. **A:** _____ Ping and Hang-Li want hot soup?

   B: Yes, they _____. They have colds.

4. **A:** _____ Alicia need aspirin?

   B: No, she _____. She needs flu medicine.

5. **A:** _____ your son feel better now?

   B: No, he _____. He has a stomachache.

PAIRS. Practice the conversations in Exercise B.

C

Write *yes / no* questions. Use the words. Then look at the pictures. Answer the questions. Use short answers.

1.

   Does Emily have a headache?
   (Emily / have / a headache)

   Yes, she does.

2.

   _____
   (Dmitri and Natasha / feel / tired)

   _____

3.

   _____
   (Khalil / want / tea)

   _____

4.

   _____
   (Mr. and Mrs. Ahn / feel / nauseous)

   _____

D

 CD 2 TRACK 15 **Listen and check your answers.**

TIME to TALK

GROUPS. Talk to your classmates. Find someone who . . .

feels tired _____	feels hot _____
feels cold _____	feels sick _____
feels hungry _____	feels thirsty _____

Write the person's name on the line.

Example:
A: *Do you feel tired?*
B: *No, I don't.*
C: *Yes, I do.*

Report to the class.

Example:
Yuri feels tired. Cecil feels . . .

Do you have a fever?

Reading and Writing

Reading

A Look at the form. Match the words on the left with the questions on the right.

> **Patient Information**
>
> Name _Joshua Pierce_
>
> Address _310 Washington Street_
>
> City _Hoboken_   State _NJ_   ZIP _07030_
>
> Sex   M _✓_ F ____ Age _32_ Soc Sec No _123-45-6789_
>
> Marital Status M ___ S _✓_ W ____ D ____ Date of Birth _4/5/74_
>
> Home Phone _201-555-3928_   Work Phone _212-555-9356_

_d_ **1.** age

____ **2.** marital status

____ **3.** date of birth

____ **4.** sex

a. When were you born?

b. Are you a man or a woman?

c. Are you married, single, widowed, or divorced?

d. How old are you?

B Write the abbreviations next to the words.

male _____   married _____   widowed _____

female _____   single _____   divorced _____

Social Security number _____

C Look at the form again. Read each sentence. Correct the mistake. Write a correct sentence.

1. Joshua Pierce is a woman.   _Joshua Pierce is a man._

2. He is 74 years old.   _____

3. He doesn't have a Social Security number.   _____

4. His date of birth is May 4, 1974.   _____

5. Joshua is married.   _____

6. His home phone number is 212-555-9356.   _____

Prewriting

Answer the questions. Use true information or made-up information.

1. What is your name? _____
2. What is your street address? _____
3. What is the abbreviation for your state? _____
4. What is your ZIP code? _____
5. Are you a man or a woman? _____
6. How old are you? _____
7. What is your social security number? _____
8. What is your marital status? _____
9. What is your date of birth? _____
10. What is your home phone number? _____
11. What is your work phone number? _____

Writing

Complete the form. Use true information or made-up information. Use the form on page 118 as a model.

Patient Information

Name _____

Address _____

City _____ State _____ ZIP_____

Sex   M _____ F _____ Age _____   Soc Sec No _____

Marital Status M ____ S _____ W _____ D _____ Date of Birth _____

Home Phone _____   Work Phone _____

Review

Put It in Place

A Complete the chart with the correct form of the verb *have*.

Subject	Verb	
I You We They	———	a fever.
He She	———	

Subject	Do / Does	Not	Verb	
I You We They	do	not	———	the flu.
He She	does			

B Complete the chart with *do*, *does*, *don't*, and *doesn't*.

Verb	Subject	
———	I you we they	feel tired?
———	he she	

	Subject	Do / Does
Yes,	you I we they	———
	he she	———

	Subject	Don't / Doesn't
No,	you I we they	———
	he she	———

Put It Together: Does She Have a Fever?

PLAYERS	2 pairs of students
MATERIALS	1 book 1 coin (Heads = move 1 box. Tails = move 2 boxes) 2 markers (1 for each pair)
GOAL	To ask and answer about how people feel
EXAMPLE	Student A, ask a question with *have* or *feel*. The answer must be No! Student A: Does Tomas have a sore throat? Student B: No he doesn't. He has a headache.
HOW TO PLAY	See page 219.

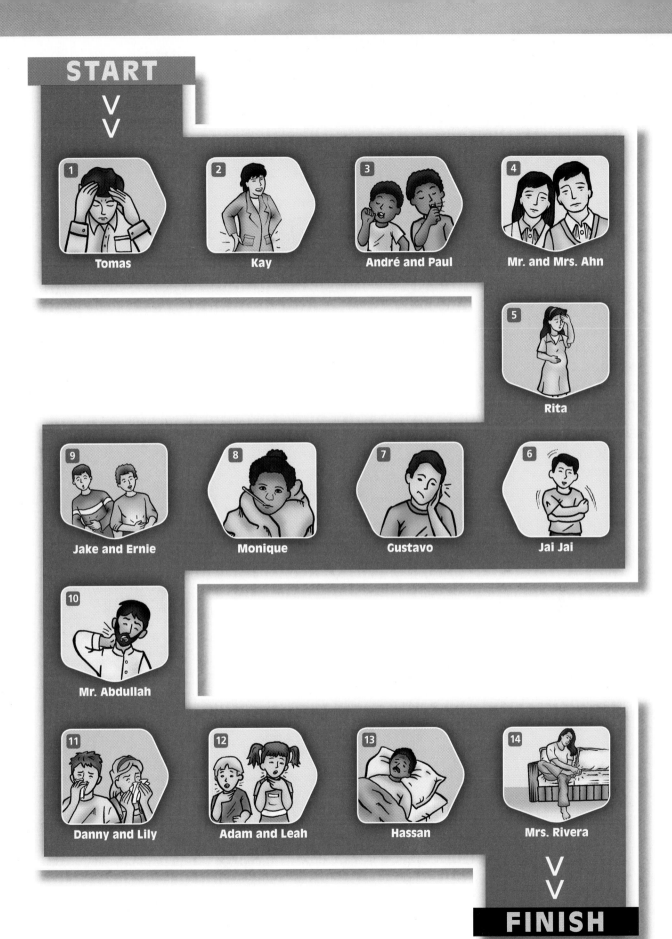

START

1 Tomas

2 Kay

3 André and Paul

4 Mr. and Mrs. Ahn

5 Rita

9 Jake and Ernie

8 Monique

7 Gustavo

6 Jai Jai

10 Mr. Abdullah

11 Danny and Lily

12 Adam and Leah

13 Hassan

14 Mrs. Rivera

FINISH

I always do the dishes.

Grammar
- Simple Present: Adverbs of Frequency
- Simple Present: Information Questions

Vocabulary

CD 2 TRACK

16 Read and listen. Then listen and repeat.

PAIRS. Look at the pictures. Check (✓) the things you do every day. Tell your partner.

Example:

A: *I get up every day! I brush my teeth. I . . .*

1. get up

2. brush your teeth

4. get dressed

5. eat breakfast

6. go to work

8. get home

9. cook dinner

10. do the dishes

Listening

Cara is on the phone with her mother.

A 🔊 CD 2 TRACK **17** Listen to the conversation. Look at the chart. What does Allan do? What does Cara do? Check (✓) the boxes.

	ALLAN	CARA
works hard		
cooks dinner		
does the dishes		
checks e-mail		

B 🔊 CD 2 TRACK **18** Listen again. Write the missing words.

Mom: How is everything, honey?

Cara: Fine, Mom. I'm just tired.

Mom: You work hard!

Cara: I know. Allan works hard, too.

Mom: Of course. Does he ever help you at home?

Cara: Sure! He sometimes _____.

We take turns.

Mom: Good. What about the dishes?

Cara: Well, uh, no, he never does the dishes.

Mom: Really?

Cara: Yes, I always _____,

and Allan checks e-mail.

Mom: I see.

3. take a shower

7. work

11. check e-mail

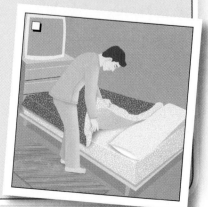

12. go to bed

I always do the dishes.   123

SIMPLE PRESENT: ADVERBS OF FREQUENCY			
Subject	Adverb of Frequency	Verb	
I You We They	always sometimes never	take a shower do the dishes go to bed	at 10:00.
He She Tom		takes a shower does the dishes goes to bed	

Look

The verbs *do* and *go* are irregular:
Jack **goes** to bed at 10:00.
Jan always **does** the dishes.

For spelling rules for 3rd person simple present verbs, see p. 213.

Look

always	100%
sometimes	↕
never	0%

A Rewrite the sentences. Use the adverb of frequency in parentheses.

1. The children get up at 7:00. (always)

   The children always get up at 7:00.

2. Mr. Garcia gets home at 6:00. (always)

   _____

3. I brush my teeth at work. (sometimes)

   _____

4. Ari eats breakfast at home. (never)

   _____

5. We check e-mail at night. (always)

   _____

6. I go to bed late. (sometimes)

   _____

7. Luc goes home at 5:00. (never)

   _____

See Pronunciation Activity A: page 207

B **Put the words in the correct order. Use capital letters as needed.**

1. _I sometimes go to bed at midnight._
   (go / at / sometimes / bed / I / midnight / to)

2. _____
   (at / father / my / night / works / sometimes)

3. _____
   (his / always / dinner / with / Claude / eats / family)

4. _____
   (home / at / Mrs. Tran / never / 5:00 / gets)

5. _____
   (their / morning / the / always / the / brush / children / teeth / in)

C **Complete the sentences. Use the words in parentheses.**

Edgardo _____always gets up_____ at 6:00 A.M. He _____
           1. (always / get up)   2. (always / brush his teeth)

and _____. He _____ coffee and toast for
      3. (take a shower)   4. (always / have)

breakfast. He _____ e-mail. Then he _____. He
           5. (never / check)   6. (get dressed)

_____ the dishes. He _____ to work at 7:00.
   7. (sometimes / do)   8. (always / go)

PAIRS. Look at the sentences. Which activities do you do always, sometimes, never? Tell your partner.

I have coffee in the morning.	I get home at 6:00.	I do the dishes.
I eat lunch at home.	I cook dinner.	I go to bed at midnight.

Example:
A: *I always have coffee in the morning.*
  I never eat lunch at home.
  I sometimes get home at 6:00. . . .

Report to the class.
B: *Lizette always has coffee in the morning. . . .*

Vocabulary and Listening

Vocabulary

19 **Read and listen. Then listen and repeat.**

PAIRS. **Look at the pictures. What do you do for fun on the weekend? Tell your partner.**

Example:

A: *I sometimes* eat out *on the weekend.*

B: *I don't* eat out*. I sometimes* get a DVD*.*

Weekend Activities

1. eat out

2. get a DVD

4. go to the movies

5. go dancing

7. relax

8. watch TV

9. go shopping

Listening

A 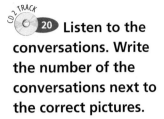 **20** **Listen to the conversations. Write the number of the conversations next to the correct pictures.**

A reporter is talking to people about weekend activities.

B **21** **Listen again. Write the missing words.**

3. visit friends

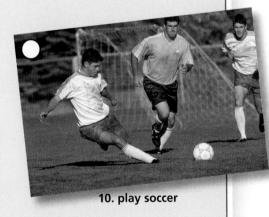

6. play cards

Conversation 1

Reporter: Hello. May I ask your name?

Natasha: Sure. It's Natasha.

Reporter: Hi, Natasha. So, what do you do for fun on the weekend?

Natasha: Oh, my friends and I _____.

Reporter: Great. How often do you go?

Natasha: Every weekend! We usually go on Friday nights.

Reporter: Really? And what time do you go?

Natasha: Around 11:00.

Conversation 2

Reporter: Hello. And your name is . . . ?

Colin: Colin.

Reporter: So, Colin, what do you do for fun on the weekend?

Colin: Oh, my girlfriend and I usually

_____.

Reporter: Great. When do you go?

Colin: We usually go on Saturday night.

Reporter: That's a popular movie night! Where do you go?

Colin: To Cinema 24, mostly. It's crowded, but it's fun.

10. play soccer

I always do the dishes.

Grammar to Communicate 2

SIMPLE PRESENT: INFORMATION QUESTIONS

Wh- word	Do / Does	Subject	Verb		
How often Where When	do	you they your parents	go	dancing?	Every weekend. At Le Club.
What time	does	he she	play	soccer?	On Saturday mornings. At 9:00.

A Complete the questions. Use the words in the box. Use each word one time.

> **Look**
>
> Saturdays = every Saturday
> Saturday mornings = every Saturday morning

How often	Where	When	What time

1. **A:** ___Where___ does Meg usually watch TV?

   B: In the living room.

2. **A:** _____ do the boys play soccer?

   B: At 9:00 on Saturday mornings.

3. **A:** _____ does Felipe visit his grandmother?

   B: Every Sunday.

4. **A:** _____ do you go food shopping?

   B: On Saturday afternoons.

B Write questions. Use the words in parentheses.

1. ___How often does Cathy eat out?_____
   (How often / Cathy / eat out)

2. _____
   (When / Rory / play soccer)

3. _____
   (Where / Mr. and Mrs. Hall / go shopping)

4. _____
   (How often / your brothers / visit you)

5. _____
   (What time / you / play cards / on Tuesdays)

See Pronunciation Activity B: page 207

C Read the answers. Look at the underlined words. Write questions with *when*, *where*, and *how often* and the words in parentheses.

1. **A:** (you) _When do you eat out?_

   B: We eat out <u>on Saturday nights</u>.

2. **A:** (Wendy) _____

   B: She goes dancing <u>at Le Club</u>.

3. **A:** (your friends) _____

   B: They <u>never</u> go to the movies. They get DVDs.

4. **A:** (Esteban) _____

   B: He visits his parents <u>on Sunday afternoons</u>.

5. **A:** (Howard and Natalie) _____

   B: They go shopping <u>at the mall</u>.

6. **A:** (Laurie) _____

   B: She watches TV <u>every night</u>.

TIME to TALK

WORK ALONE. Write four questions about weekend activities.

QUESTION	CLASSMATE 1	CLASSMATE 2
When do you visit your friends?	on Sundays	on Friday nights
When		
Where		
How often		
What time		

GROUPS. Take turns asking your questions. Write your classmates' answers in the chart.

Example:
A: *When do you visit your friends?*
B: *I visit my friends on Sundays.*
C: *I visit my friends on Friday nights.*

Report to the class.

Example:
Min-Jee visits her friends on Sundays. Aida visits her friends on Friday nights.

I always do the dishes.   129

Reading and Writing

Reading

A Look at the graph. What does the graph show?

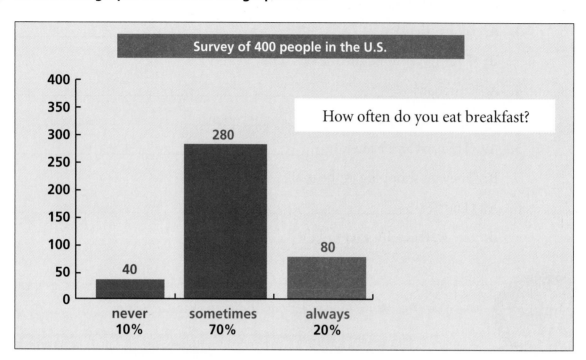

Survey of 400 people in the U.S.

How often do you eat breakfast?

never	sometimes	always
10%	70%	20%

40 280 80

B Write sentences about the survey.

1. *Forty people never eat breakfast.*

   10% never eat breakfast.

2. _____

   _____

3. _____

   _____

Prewriting

A Take a survey of the class. Ask, *How often do you eat breakfast?* Complete the chart with the number of people in each category.

never _____

sometimes _____

always _____

B Make a graph with the information from Exercise A.

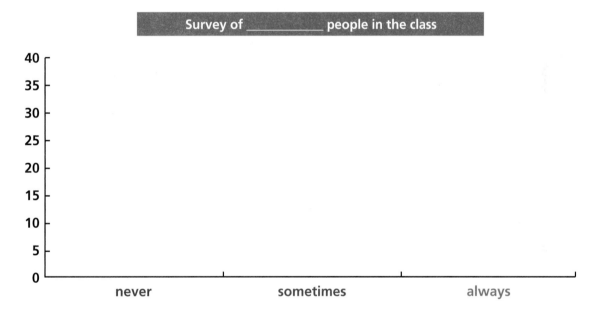

Survey of _____ people in the class

40		
35		
30		
25		
20		
15		
10		
5		
0		
never	sometimes	always

Writing

Write sentences about the survey. Use the sentences on page 130 as a model.

1. _____

_____

2. _____

_____

3. _____

_____

Review

Put It in Place

A   Write three sentences about people you know using *always*, *sometimes*, and *never*. Use these verb phrases: *eat lunch at school, do the dishes, go to bed at 11:00*.

1. _____ always _____.
2. _____ sometimes _____.
3. _____ never _____.

B   Complete the chart. Use one of these verb phrases: *watch TV, eat out, go shopping*.

Wh- word	Do / Does	Subject	Verb
How often Where When	_____	you they	
	_____	he she	_____?

Put It Together: Where? When? What Time? How Often?

PLAYERS	2 pairs of students
MATERIALS	1 book 1 coin (Heads = move 1 box. Tails = move 2 boxes) 2 markers (1 for each pair)
GOAL	To ask and answer questions with *where, when, what time,* and *how often*
EXAMPLE	Student A: How often do you check e-mail? Student B: I check e-mail every day.
HOW TO PLAY	See page 220.

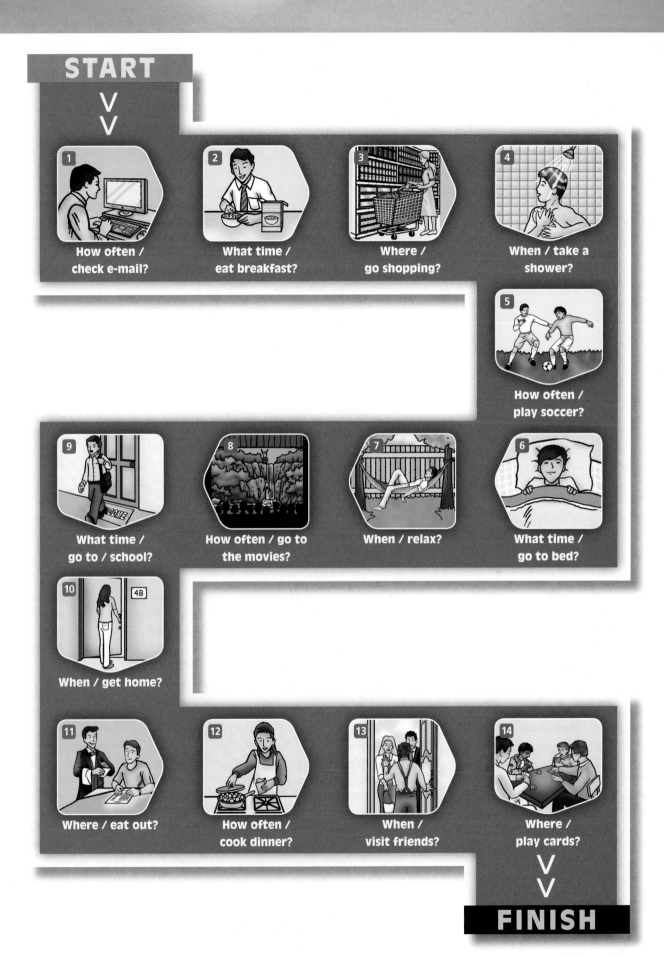

START

1. How often / check e-mail?
2. What time / eat breakfast?
3. Where / go shopping?
4. When / take a shower?
5. How often / play soccer?
6. What time / go to bed?
7. When / relax?
8. How often / go to the movies?
9. What time / go to / school?
10. When / get home?
11. Where / eat out?
12. How often / cook dinner?
13. When / visit friends?
14. Where / play cards?

FINISH

I always do the dishes.   133

Unit 12
It's next to the bank.

Grammar
- Prepositions of Location
- Object Pronouns: *It* and *Them*

Vocabulary

22 **Read and listen. Then listen and repeat.**

1. parking lot
2. hospital
3. bank
4. coffee shop
5. restaurant
6. park
7. library
8. gas station
9. post office
10. apartment building
11. department store
12. firehouse
13. movie theater
14. police station

PAIRS. Student A, ask about places in Student B's neighborhood. Student B, give true answers. Take turns.

Example:

A: *Is there a coffee shop in your neighborhood?*

B: *Yes, there is—Two Brothers Coffee Shop.*

Listening

Abdir and Noel are talking about
Noel's new neighborhood.

A CD 2 TRACK **23** Listen to the conversation. Check (✓) the
places in the picture you hear.

B CD 2 TRACK **24** Listen again. Write the missing words.

Abdir: Do you like your new neighborhood?

Noel: Yes, I do. It's very convenient. There are a lot

of stores near my apartment building.

Abdir: Oh, really?

Noel: Uh-huh. And there's a _____ right

around the corner, on Park Avenue.

Abdir: That's great.

Noel: Yeah, and next to the bank, there's a

_____.

Abdir: Oh, yeah?

Noel: Yeah. And there's a _____

across the street from my building.

Abdir: Terrific! Where's your apartment, again?

Noel: It's on the corner of Jefferson Street and

Garden Avenue.

It's next to the bank. 135

Grammar to Communicate 1

PREPOSITIONS OF LOCATION

Prepositions of location with street names

The police station is **on** Railroad Avenue.
The gas station is **on the corner of** Main Street and Railroad Avenue.

Prepositions of location with places

The restaurant is **next to** the park.
The parking lot is **across from** the gas station.

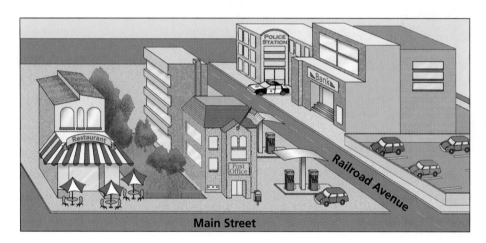

Main Street

A   Look at the picture. Fill in the blank. Use *next to*, *on*, *on the corner of*,
or *across from*.

1. The police station is _____ *next to* _____ the bank.

2. The restaurant is _____ Main Street.

3. The bank is _____ the parking lot.

4. The parking lot is _____ Main Street and Railroad Avenue.

5. The gas station is _____ the parking lot.

B   Look at the picture. Complete the sentences with the places.
Sometimes there can be more than one correct answer.

1. The ___ *post office* ___ is next to the park. OR The ___ *restaurant* ___ is next to the park.

2. The _____ is across from the gas station.

3. The _____ is on Main Street.

4. The _____ is on the corner of Main Street and Railroad Avenue.

5. The _____ is on Railroad Avenue.

C Look at the picture. Answer the questions. (There may be more than one correct answer.)

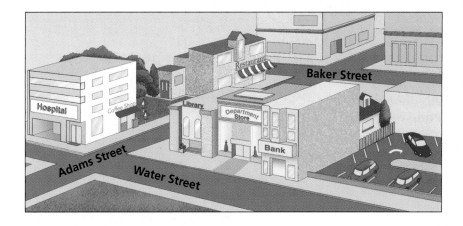

1. **A:** Excuse me. Is there a park near here?

   B: Yes. There's ___a park on Adams Street. It's next to the restaurant___ .

2. **A:** Excuse me. Is there a library near here?

   B: Yes. There's _____ .

3. **A:** Excuse me. Is there a restaurant near here?

   B: Yes. There's _____ .

4. **A:** Excuse me. Is there a bank near here?

   B: Yes. There's _____ .

5. **A:** Excuse me. Is there a hospital near here?

   B: Yes. There's _____ .

D 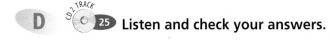 **Listen and check your answers.**

PAIRS. **Practice the conversations.**

WORK ALONE. **Think about places near your school, such as a police station, a restaurant, a bank, and a park. Draw a map.**

PAIRS. **Ask your partner questions about the places. Take turns.**

Example:
A: *Is there a police station near here?*
B: *Yes. There's a police station on Sutter Street. It's next to a bank.*

Vocabulary and Listening

Vocabulary

CD 2 TRACK **26** Read and listen. Then listen and repeat.

PAIRS. Practice the conversation. Then make a new conversation. Use true information.

Example:
A: *Where do you get eggs?*
B: *At the supermarket. What about you?*

1. discount store

2. convenience store

3. supermarket

4. grocery store

5. drugstore

6. eggs

7. milk

8. meat

9. fish

10. chicken

11. vegetables

12. fruit

13. cookies

14. toothpaste

15. soap

138   Unit 12

Listening

A 🔘 **27** **Listen to the conversation. Answer the question. Circle the letter of the correct reason.**

Why does the woman shop at the supermarket?

a. The supermarket has everything for her family.

b. The supermarket is near her house.

c. The supermarket is open late.

An interviewer for a radio show asks a shopper about her shopping habits.

B 🔘 **28** **Listen again. Fill in the missing words.**

Interviewer: Excuse me, ma'am. Can I ask you a question or two?

Shopper: OK.

Interviewer: Do you usually get all your groceries at the supermarket?

Shopper: Yes. Everyone in my family has favorite foods and the supermarket has everything.

Interviewer: Everything?

Shopper: Yes. For example, my daughter likes chocolate chip _____ and I buy them there.

Interviewer: I see.

Shopper: And my son likes a special kind of _____ and the supermarket always has it.

Interviewer: So you shop at the supermarket because it has everything?

Shopper: Yes. Oh, and the prices are good. That's very important.

Grammar to Communicate 2

OBJECT PRONOUNS: *IT* AND *THEM*

	Object Noun		Object Pronoun	
My son likes	pizza.	He eats	it	every day.
We like	vegetables.	We eat	them	every day.

A Match the sentences on the left with the sentences on the right.

_d_ **1.** My kids like ice cream.

_____ **2.** Celia buys cookies at the drugstore.

_____ **3.** I cook vegetables every night.

_____ **4.** Dan likes Crown soap.

_____ **5.** We never have coffee at night.

a. We always have it in the morning.

b. He gets it at Shop 'n Shop.

c. She buys them on sale.

d. They have it for dessert every night.

e. I cook them in the microwave.

B Complete the conversations. Use *it* or *them*.

1. **A:** Marie likes chocolate cake.

  B: I know. She has ____it____ every day for dessert.

2. **A:** How often do you eat eggs?

  B: We have _____ two times a week.

3. **A:** Do you eat breakfast every day?

  B: Yes, but sometimes I have _____ at work.

4. **A:** Do you need those spoons?

  B: No, you can use _____.

5. **A:** Do your kids like fish?

  B: No, they never eat _____.

6. **A:** Do you want hamburgers tonight?

  B: OK. Let's have _____ with French fries.

C CD 2 TRACK 29 Listen and check your answers.

PAIRS. Practice the conversations in Exercise B.

 See Pronunciation Activity B: page 208

D **Complete the sentences. Use *it* and *them*.**

1. There's no milk. We need _____it_____ for the children.

2. We eat apples every day. I buy _____ every week at the supermarket.

3. My daughter likes pizza. We always have _____ for dinner on the weekend.

4. Do you like eggs? Yes. I like _____ for breakfast on Sundays.

5. We sometimes have fish for dinner. We buy _____ fresh.

6. Larry likes hot dogs. He gets _____ for lunch at the hot dog stand.

7. My children don't like green vegetables. Do your children like _____?

8. Do you like milk and sugar in your coffee? No, I like _____ black.

WORK ALONE. **Look at the items in the chart. Do you buy them? Where do you buy them? Write your answers in the column for Student A.**

	STUDENT A	STUDENT B	STUDENT C
cookies			
eggs			
meat, fish, and chicken			
fruit			
vegetables			
milk			
soap and toothpaste			

GROUPS OF 3. **Take a survey. Ask each other the questions about each item. Ask, *Do you buy . . . ?/ Where do you buy . . . ?* Write the answers.**

Example:
A: *Do you buy cookies?*
B: *Yes, I do.*
A: *Where do you buy them?*
B: *I buy them at the convenience store.*

Report to the class.

Example:
Joon buys cookies at the convenience store.
Blanca buys them at the drugstore. I buy
them at the supermarket.

Reading and Writing

Reading

A   **Read the e-mail. Noel is writing to his friend about his new neighborhood.**

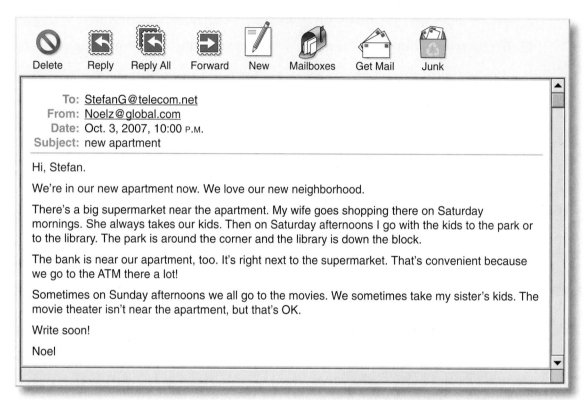

To: StefanG@telecom.net
From: Noelz@global.com
Date: Oct. 3, 2007, 10:00 P.M.
Subject: new apartment

Hi, Stefan.

We're in our new apartment now. We love our new neighborhood.

There's a big supermarket near the apartment. My wife goes shopping there on Saturday mornings. She always takes our kids. Then on Saturday afternoons I go with the kids to the park or to the library. The park is around the corner and the library is down the block.

The bank is near our apartment, too. It's right next to the supermarket. That's convenient because we go to the ATM there a lot!

Sometimes on Sunday afternoons we all go to the movies. We sometimes take my sister's kids. The movie theater isn't near the apartment, but that's OK.

Write soon!

Noel

B   **Read the e-mail again. Read the sentences. They all have mistakes. Cross out the mistake. Write the correction.**

                   neighborhood
1. Noel is happy in his new ~~job~~.

2. There's a big discount store near his apartment.

3. Noel and his kids go shopping at the supermarket on Saturday mornings.

4. On Saturday afternoons, Noel takes his kids to school or to the library.

5. The park is across the street from his apartment.

6. The bank is near his apartment. It's across the street from the supermarket.

7. They always go to the movies on Sunday afternoons.

8. The movie theater is near their apartment.

Prewriting

Draw a map of your neighborhood. Use the map on page 134 as a model.

Writing

Write an e-mail about your neighborhood. Use the map. Use Noel's e-mail on page 142 as a model.

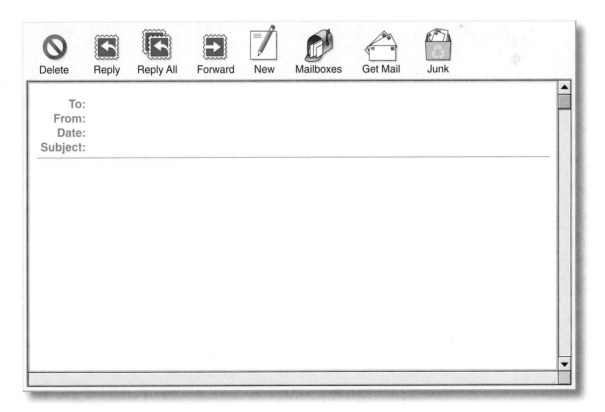

| Delete | Reply | Reply All | Forward | New | Mailboxes | Get Mail | Junk |

To:
From:
Date:
Subject:

Put It in Place

Read the sentences. Write the names of the places on the map.

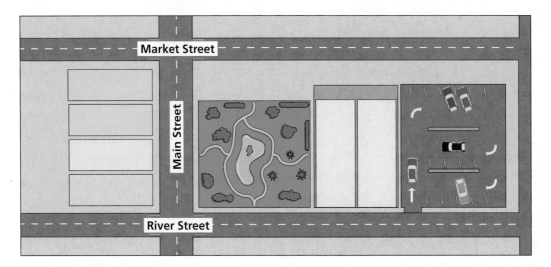

There's a drugstore on the corner of Main Street and River Street. It's next to the discount store. There's a coffee shop on the corner of Main Street and Market Street. There's a police station next to the coffee shop. There's a park on the corner of Main Street and River Street. There's a supermarket on River Street next to the park. There's a restaurant next to the supermarket. There's a parking lot next to the restaurant.

Put It Together: City Planners Project

PLAYERS	2 students
MATERIALS	1 book
GOAL	To plan a city
EXAMPLE	Student A: Put the park on Market Street. Student B: What about on California Avenue?
HOW TO PLAY	See page 220.

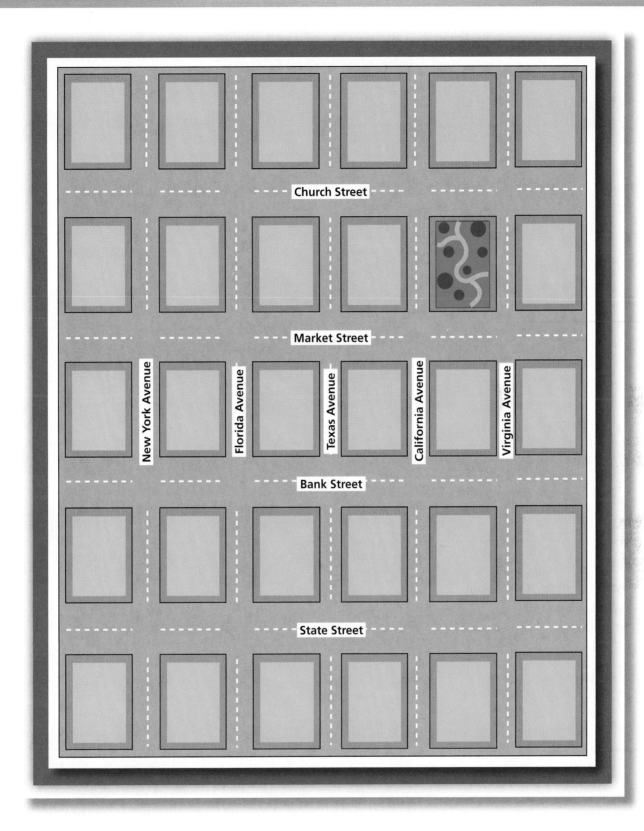

Church Street

Market Street

New York Avenue

Florida Avenue

Texas Avenue

California Avenue

Virginia Avenue

Bank Street

State Street

Unit 13
I'm talking on the phone.

Grammar
- Present Progressive: Affirmative Statements
- Present Progressive: Negative Statements

Vocabulary

30 **Read and listen. Then listen and repeat.**

1. sleep
2. help someone
3. play video games
4. listen to music
5. talk on the phone
6. drink coffee
7. watch TV
8. read the newspaper
9. study

PAIRS. **Practice the conversation. Talk about what you do in your free time. Use the words above.**

Example:

A: *What do you do in your free time?*

B: *I listen to music! What about you?*

1.

2.

4.

5.

7.

8.

Listening

A CD 2 TRACK **31** Listen to the conversations. Check (✓) the correct picture for each person.

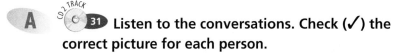

father			
son			
Emma			

B CD 2 TRACK **32** Listen again. Fill in the missing words.

Conversation 1

Son: Dad, are you busy?

Father: Not really. I'm reading the newspaper.

Son: Oh, yeah. You _____ the newspaper every night.

Father: That's right. So, what's up?

Son: I'm studying for a test. Can you _____ me?

Father: Of course! What's the subject?

Son: English.

Father: Uh, where's your mother?

Conversation 2

Mom: Where's your sister Emma? It's 6:30—time for dinner.

Son: I bet she's talking on her cell phone.

Mom: You're probably right. She and her friends _____ on the phone all the time. Look in her room.

Son: No, she isn't there, Mom.

Mom: Is she in the living room?

Son: Yup. She's sleeping on the sofa!

3.

6.

9.

I'm talking on the phone. 147

Grammar to Communicate 1

PRESENT PROGRESSIVE: AFFIRMATIVE STATEMENTS

Subject	Be	Verb + -ing	Contractions		
I	am		I	+ am → I'm	
He She Jack	is	studying.	He She	+ is →	He's She's
You We They	are		You We They	+ are →	You're We're They're

Look

Use the present progressive to describe an action that is happening now.

For spelling rules for the *-ing* form of the verb, see p. 213.

A Complete the sentences. Use the verbs in parentheses. Use contractions.

1. **A:** Where is Kevin?

   B: He's in his bedroom. He <u>'s studying</u>.
   (study)

2. **A:** Where are Helena and Sara?

   B: They're in their room. They _____ e-mail.
   (check)

3. **A:** Where are you?

   B: I'm in the living room. I _____ to music.
   (listen)

4. **A:** Where are Dan and Maggie?

   B: They're in the bedroom. They _____ video games.
   (play)

5. **A:** Where is Andrea?

   B: She _____. Be quiet!
   (sleep)

6. **A:** Where are you and Marie?

   B: We're in the kitchen. We _____ Rose with her homework.
   (help)

B CD 2 TRACK 33 **Listen and check your answers.**

PAIRS. **Practice the conversations in Exercise A.**

Look at the pictures. Write a sentence to describe each one. Write two sentences for items 5 and 6.

1.

Alex

Robbie

Alex is helping Robbie with his toy.

2.

Mr. Clark

_____

3.

Ming

Janie

_____

4.

Mr. and Mrs. Moon

_____

5.

Ms. Curtis

_____

_____

6.

Pedro

_____

_____

TIME to TALK

PAIRS. **Student A, act out an action. Use the verbs in the box. Student B, guess the action. Take turns.**

check e-mail	read
drink coffee	sleep
listen to music	study
play	talk on the phone

Example:
B: *You're studying.*
A: *No!*
B: *You're reading a book.*
A: *Yes!*

I'm talking on the phone.

Vocabulary and Listening

Vocabulary

CD 2 TRACK 34 **Read and listen. Then listen and repeat.**

1. clean the house
2. do homework
3. make the bed
4. get the mail
5. fix the door
6. watch the children
7. take care of the plants
8. take out the trash
9. do the laundry

PAIRS. **Look at the picture. What do you do at home? Tell your partner. Take turns.**

Example:
A: *I clean the house.*
B: *I clean the house, too. And I take out the trash.*

Listening

Mrs. Soto is talking to Luis.

A CD 2 TRACK 35 **Listen to the conversation. Then complete the sentence. Circle the correct letter.**

Eric is _____

a. checking e-mail

b. cleaning his room

c. playing video games

B CD 2 TRACK 36 **Listen again. Fill in the missing words.**

Luis: Hi, Mrs. Soto. Is Eric home?

Mrs. Soto: Yes, he is. He's making his _____.

He _____ his bed every morning.

Eric? Luis is here. What are you doing?

Eric: Wait, Mom. Don't come in.

Mrs. Soto: Eric! You aren't making your bed! You're playing video games!

Eric: I'm not playing video games, Mom. I'm checking e-mail.

Grammar to Communicate 2

PRESENT PROGRESSIVE: NEGATIVE STATEMENTS

Subject	*Be*	*Not*	Verb + *-ing*	Contractions
I	am			
He She Kevin	is	not	cleaning.	Is + not → **Isn't** Are + not → **Aren't**
You We They	are			

Look

Spelling changes
make + *-ing* = *making*
get + *-ing* = *getting*

For spelling rules for the *-ing* form of the verb, see p. 213.

A Look at the pictures. Complete the sentences. Use the verbs in parentheses. Then write a sentence to describe the picture.

1. Sabine ____isn't getting____ the mail.
   (not get)

   She's cleaning the house.

2. Kyle and Joe _____ their homework.
   (not do)

   _____

3. Ivan _____ e-mail.
   (not check)

   _____

4. I _____ the trash.
   (not take out)

   _____

5. We _____ the house.
   (not clean)

   _____

See Pronunciation Activity B: page 209

B Complete the conversations. Use the verbs in parentheses. Then write a negative and affirmative sentence. Use contractions.

1. **A:** Arturo is in the living room. He <u>'s fixing</u> the TV.
   (fix)

   B: He <u>isn't / He's not fixing the TV</u>. He <u>'s taking out</u> the trash.
   (take out)

2. **A:** Katerina is outside. I think she _____ the mail.
   (get)

   B: She _____. She _____ for food.
   (shop)

3. **A:** Manny isn't here. I think he _____ the laundry.
   (do)

   B: He _____. He _____ the plants.
   (take care of)

4. **A:** Patrice and Michel _____ the house.
   (clean)

   B: They _____. They _____ the kids.
   (watch)

TIME to TALK

PAIRS. **Look at the pictures. Student A, choose one person (but don't tell Student B). Say three things about what the person** *isn't* **doing. Student B, guess who it is. Take turns.**

Example:
A: *She isn't doing the laundry. She isn't making the bed. She isn't getting the mail.*
B: *Is it Yolanda?*
A: *No! Guess again!*

Victoria

Yolanda

Serena

Abby

Wei-Wei

Kyung-A

Reading and Writing

Reading

A Read the e-mail. Alex is writing to a friend. What is he writing about?

_____

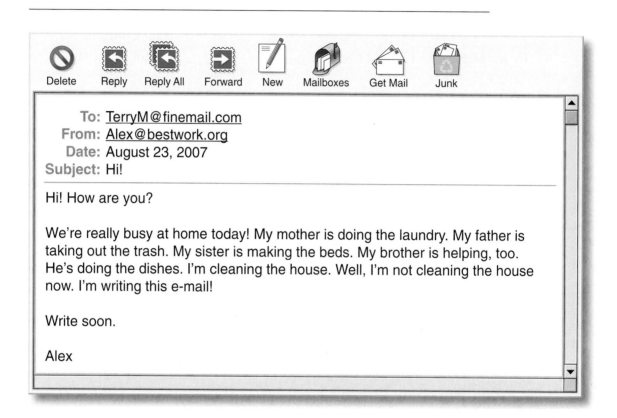

To: TerryM@finemail.com
From: Alex@bestwork.org
Date: August 23, 2007
Subject: Hi!

Hi! How are you?

We're really busy at home today! My mother is doing the laundry. My father is taking out the trash. My sister is making the beds. My brother is helping, too. He's doing the dishes. I'm cleaning the house. Well, I'm not cleaning the house now. I'm writing this e-mail!

Write soon.

Alex

B Read the e-mail again. Match the parts of the sentences.

_c_ **1.** Alex's mother   **a.** is doing the dishes.

____ **2.** His father   **b.** isn't cleaning the house.

____ **3.** His sister   **c.** is doing the laundry.

____ **4.** His brother   **d.** is taking out the trash.

____ **5.** Alex   **e.** is making the beds.

PAIRS. **Compare answers.**

Prewriting

Alex's family is not busy now. What is each person doing now? Choose one verb for each person in Alex's family. Complete the sentences.

check e-mail	listen to music	sleep
drink coffee	play video games	talk on the phone
eat	read	watch TV

1. Alex's mother _____

2. Alex's father _____

3. Alex's sister _____

4. Alex's brother _____

5. Alex _____

Writing

You are Alex. Write a new e-mail to Terry. Use your sentences from Prewriting.

Delete   Reply   Reply All   Forward   New   Mailboxes   Get Mail   Junk

To: TerryM@finemail.com
From: Alex@bestwork.org
Date: August 23, 2007
Subject: Hi!

Hi! How are you?

We're relaxing at home today! My mother _____.

My father _____. My sister _____.

My brother _____. He's _____.

I _____. Well, I _____ now. I'm

writing this e-mail!

Write soon.

Alex

Review

Put It in Place

Complete the charts with the present progressive. Use the verb *read* in the affirmative and *sleep* in the negative.

Affirmative		
I	_____	
He She	_____	_____
You We They	_____	

Negative			
I	_____		
He She	_____	not	_____
You We They	_____		

Put It Together: Four in a Row

PLAYERS	2 students
MATERIALS	1 book
GOAL	To make sentences about what people are doing
EXAMPLE	Number 1. Igor is watching TV. Number 3. Elena is not doing the laundry.
HOW TO PLAY	See page 220.

1 Igor
2 Kyung
3 Cathy
4 Elena
5 Mr. Barber
6 Mr. and Mrs. Gomez
7 Mike
8 Ana, Grace, Mona
9 Tammy
10 Andy, Charlie, Lee
11 Liz
12 Kurt and Tommy
13 Gwen and Mary
14 Amélie
15 Pat and Dana
16 Eric

Vocabulary

CD 2 TRACK 37 Read and listen. Then listen and repeat.

1. park the car
2. walk
3. take a taxi
4. take the subway
5. take the train
6. take the bus
7. wait for the light
8. drive
9. cross the street
10. ride my bike

PAIRS. **Practice the conversation. Then make a new conversation. Talk about yourself.**

Example:

A: *I take the bus to school. What about you?*

B: *I drive.*

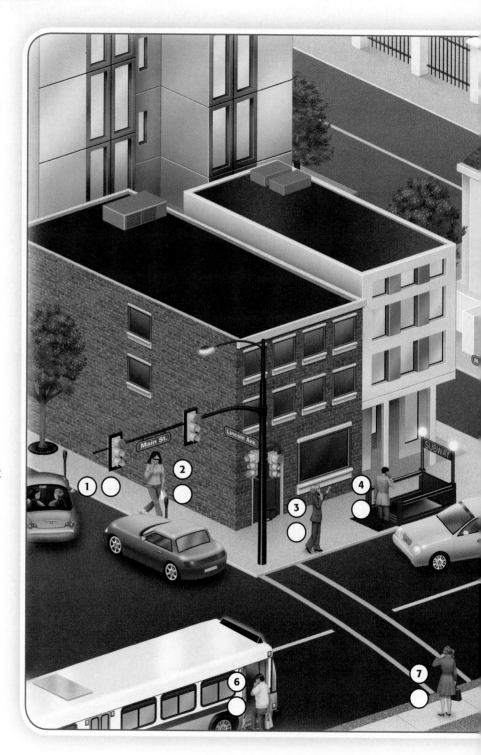

Listening

A **38** Listen to the conversations. Write the number of the conversations next to the correct person in the picture.

B **39** Listen again. Fill in the missing words.

The people are talking on their cell phones.

Conversation 1

A: Hi. Where are you?

B: I'm on my way to school.

A: Are you taking the _____?

B: No, I'm not. I'm riding my _____.

A: Well, don't talk on the phone! Be careful!

Conversation 2

A: Hi. Where are you?

B: We're in the _____.

A: Is Henry driving?

B: Yes, he is.

A: Are you wearing your seat belt?

B: Of course!

Conversation 3

A: Hi. Where are you?

B: We're on our way to school.

A: Are you taking the _____?

B: No, we're not. We're taking the _____.

A: Oh, OK.

Are you walking to school? **159**

Grammar to Communicate 1

PRESENT PROGRESSIVE: *YES / NO* QUESTIONS AND SHORT ANSWERS

Be	Subject	Verb + *-ing*							
Am	I			you	are.			you	are not.
Is	she	driving now?	Yes,	she	is.	No,		she	is not.
				I	am.			I	am not.
Are	you			you	are.			you	are not.

Contractions		
No, I am not	→ No, I'm not.	
No, you are not	→ No, you aren't.	OR No, you're not.
No, we are not	→ No, we aren't.	OR No, we're not.
No, they are not	→ No, they aren't.	OR No, they're not.
No, he is not	→ No, he isn't.	OR No, he's not.

A Put the words in the correct order to make questions. Use capital letters as needed.

1. _Is Tom taking the bus to school?_____
    (taking / bus / Tom / is / to / the / school)

2. _____
    (Ms. Salas / the / crossing / is / street)

3. _____
    (the children / waiting / the / for / are / light)

4. _____
    (subway / to / you / taking / are / the / work)

5. _____
    (is / the / George / car / parking)

6. _____
    (a / taking / are / taxi / Mr. and Mrs. Gray)

B Complete the conversations. Use the words in parentheses.

1. **A:** (take the train) _____ you _____? **B:** Yes, I _____.

2. **A:** (drive to school) _____ you _____? **B:** Yes, we _____.

3. **A:** (ride your bike) _____ you _____? **B:** No, I _____.

4. **A:** (take the bus) _____ you _____? **B:** No, we _____.

See Pronunciation Activity A: page 210

C Use the words in parentheses to write questions. Look at the pictures and give short answers. Then write another sentence about the picture.

1. A: Is Debra taking the bus?
   (Debra / take the bus?)

   B: No, she isn't. OR No, she's not.

   She's riding her bike.

2. A: _____
   (Len / take a taxi?)

   B: _____

   _____

3. A: _____
   (Mr. and Mrs. Owens / walk?)

   B: _____

   _____

4. A: _____
   (Noemi / wait for the light?)

   B: _____

   _____

5. A: _____
   (Ms. Chen and her son / drive?)

   B: _____

   _____

PAIRS. Look at the pictures in Exercise C. Student A, ask a *yes / no* question about the person or people. The answer must be *No!* Student B, answer the question. Add a sentence with the correct name. Take turns.

Example:
A: *Is Debra driving?*
B: *No, she isn't. Len is driving.*

Vocabulary

 40 **Read and listen. Then listen and repeat.**

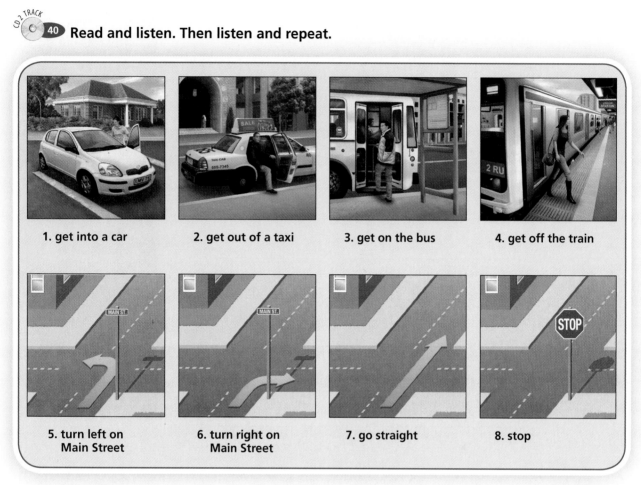

1. get into a car
2. get out of a taxi
3. get on the bus
4. get off the train

5. turn left on Main Street
6. turn right on Main Street
7. go straight
8. stop

PAIRS. Look at the transportation words in the box. Write the words near the verbs they can go with.

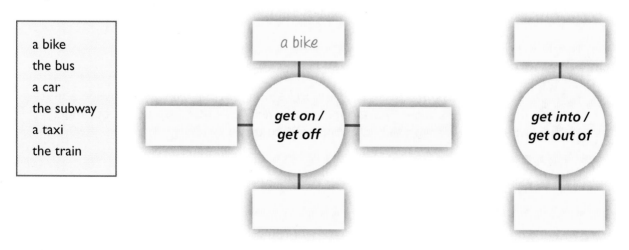

a bike
the bus
a car
the subway
a taxi
the train

a bike

get on / get off

get into / get out of

Listening

Two police officers are following a car. They think the car is stolen.

A CD 2 TRACK 41 **Listen to the conversations. Check (✓) the correct map.**

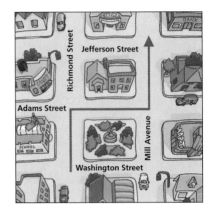

_____ a.

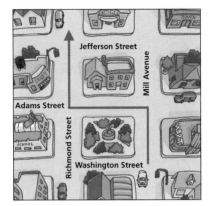

_____ b.

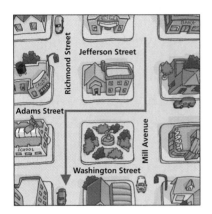

_____ c.

B CD 2 TRACK 42 **Listen again. Write the missing words.**

Conversation Part 1

Officer 1: Who's driving the _____?

Officer 2: The driver is a man. He's about 20 years old.

Officer 1: Look! He's going straight on Mill Avenue.

Officer 2: What's he doing now?

Officer 1: He's turning _____ on Adams Street.

Officer 2: No, wait. Now he's turning _____ on Richmond Street.

Officer 1: Where is he going now?

Officer 2: He's going _____ on Richmond Street.

Conversation Part 2

Officer 2: Now he's stopping. Why is he stopping?

Officer 1: He's parking the _____. Let's go!

Officer 2: Get out of the car! Hands up!

Young man: What's the problem, officer?

Officer 1: You're driving a stolen car.

Young man: No, I'm not! This is my mother's car!

Are you walking to school? **163**

Grammar to Communicate 2

PRESENT PROGRESSIVE: INFORMATION QUESTIONS

Wh- questions					Contractions
Wh- Word	Be	Subject	Verb + -ing		Who + is ⟶ Who's
Who	is	she	waiting for?	She's waiting for her friend.	What + is ⟶ What's
What	are	they	doing?	They're turning left.	
When	is	Tony	going?	He's going at 9:00.	
Where	are	you	going?	I'm going to work.	

Wh- questions About the Subject				
Who	is		driving?	A man is driving.
What			happening?	The car is stopping.

A   **Choose the correct question word. Then look at the pictures. Write answers.**

1. A: ___*Where*___ are you going?
   (What / Where)

   B: ___*I'm going to Shop 'n Shop.*___

2. A: _____ is driving?
   (Who / Where)

   B: _____

3. A: _____ are the kids doing?
   (Where / What)

   B: _____

4. A: _____ are you waiting for?
   (Who / Where)

   B: _____

5. A: _____ is she turning?
   (Where / Who)

   B: _____

See Pronunciation Activity B: page 210

B   **Read the answers. Write questions. Use the words in parentheses.**

1. **A:** (Where) _Where are you going?_____

   B: We're going to work.

2. **A:** (Who) _____

   B: My father is driving.

3. **A:** (What) _____

   B: He's driving a dark blue car.

4. **A:** (Where) _____

   B: She's getting off near her house.

5. **A:** (Who) _____

   B: They're going with their parents.

6. **A:** (What) _____

   B: She's walking to work.

C   **Listen and check your answers.**

PAIRS. **Read the sentences. Ask two or more questions for each sentence.**

Example:
Juan and Dario are getting into a taxi.
A: *Who's getting into a taxi?*
B: *What are Juan and Dario doing?*

1. Mr. Benet is waiting for his wife.

2. The police officer is talking to the driver.

3. Shanta is going straight on Main Street.

4. Mikhail and Natalia are taking the train at Grand Central Station.

5. Ahmed is parking on River Road.

6. Hye-Kyung is driving to school.

7. Mr. and Mrs. Ross are riding their bikes in the park.

Reading and Writing

Reading

 A   **Malena is writing an e-mail to her friend Greg. Read the e-mail. Can you picture Malena's street?**

> **To:** GregB@cheapmail.com
> **From:** Malena@grouptalk.net
> **Date:** Nov. 12, 2008, 3 P.M.
> **Subject:** Re: Looking out the window
>
> Dear Greg,
>
> I'm sitting in my bedroom. I'm looking out the window. There are a lot of people on the street. A man is crossing the street. He's wearing a blue jacket. A red car is turning left on King Street. A police officer is talking to two little kids. A woman is parking her car. An old man and woman are waiting for the light. Two young women are getting into a yellow taxi.
>
> Where is everyone going?

B   **Answer the questions about the e-mail. Write complete sentences.**

1. What is Malena doing?

   Malena is sitting in her bedroom. She's looking out the window. She's writing

   an e-mail.

2. Who is crossing the street?

   _____

3. Where is the red car turning?

   _____

4. Who is the police officer talking to?

   _____

5. Is a man parking his car?

   _____

6. Who is waiting for the light?

   _____

7. Are the young women getting into a car?

   _____

Prewriting

Imagine you are looking out a window in your house. There are a lot of people on the street. Draw a picture of the street.

PAIRS. Show your picture to your partner. Tell your partner about the people in your picture.

Example:

A man is riding his bike. He's wearing a black shirt.

Writing

Write an e-mail to a friend about the people on the street. Use the e-mail on page 166 as a model.

To:
From:
Date:
Subject: Re: Looking out the window

Dear _____,

I'm sitting in my _____ and I'm looking out the window. There are a lot of

people on the street. _____

_____

_____

_____

_____

Put It in Place

A Complete the charts with the correct form of the verb *be*. Use capital letters as needed.

Yes / No Questions				Short Answers						
_____	I				you	_____.		you	_____ not.
_____	he	walking now?	Yes,	he	_____.	No,	he	_____ not.
_____	they				they	_____.		they	_____ not.

B Complete the charts. Use *Who*, *What*, and *Where*.

Wh- Questions			Wh- Questions About the Subject		
_____	is	she talking to?	_____	is	talking?
_____	are	they getting off?	_____		happening?
_____	are	you doing?			

Put It Together: What's Happening?

PLAYERS	2 pairs of students
MATERIALS	1 book 1 coin (Heads = move 1 box. Tails = move 2 boxes) 2 markers (1 for each pair)
GOAL	To ask and answer about what people are doing
EXAMPLE	Student A: Who's crossing the street? Student B: Bill is crossing the street.
HOW TO PLAY	See page 221.

START

FINISH

Who?

What?

Where?

Yes / No?

Who?

What?

Where?

Yes / No?

Yes / No?

Where?

What?

Who?

Yes / No?

Where?

What?

Who?

Grace

Megan

Dylan and Cristina

Julia

Richard

Ani

Max and Brian

Luis

Taylor

Bill

Unit 15
My boyfriend can't sing.

Grammar
- *Can* for Ability: Statements
- *Can* for Ability: *Yes / No* Questions
- *Can* for Ability: Information Questions

Vocabulary

 44 Read and listen. Then listen and repeat.

PAIRS. Practice the conversation. Then make a new conversation. Use true information.

Example:
A: *Do you have any hobbies?*
B: *Yes. I bake. What about you?*
A: *I work in my garden.*

Talents and Hobbies

1. sing

2. dance

4. tell jokes

5. draw

7. knit

8. sew

9. bake

Listening

 A  Listen to the conversation. Check (✓) what Jane's boyfriend can do.

Kate and Jane are talking about Jane's boyfriend.

3. play the guitar

6. paint

B  Listen again. Fill in the missing words.

Kate: What's your boyfriend like?

Jane: He's very funny. He can _____ jokes and funny stories.

Kate: Oh, really?

Jane: Yes, and he's talented, too.

Kate: Oh, yeah?

Jane: Yeah. He can _____ the guitar and sing.

Kate: Wow! Is he a good cook, too?

Jane: Oh, no. He can't _____. And he can't _____ things. He's not good with machines.

Kate: That's OK. Does he have a brother?

10. work in your garden

My boyfriend can't sing.

171

Grammar to Communicate 1

CAN FOR ABILITY: STATEMENTS

Affirmative			Negatives					Contraction
Subject	*Can*	Verb	Subject	*Can*	*Not*	Verb		
I You He She We They Sara and Matt	can	sing.	I You He She We They Sara and Matt	can	not	dance.		Can + not ⟶ **Can't**

A Look at the pictures. Complete the sentences with *can* or *can't* and a verb in the box.

> **Look**
> We hardly ever use *cannot*.

| bake | knit | paint | play the guitar | sew | tell jokes |

1.

Mr. Leu _____*can sew*_____.

2.

Danielle _____.

3.

Fabio _____.

4.

Grace _____.

5.

Henry _____.

6.

Wendy and Alicia

_____.

See Pronunciation Activity A: page 211

B Write a new sentence. Use the verb in parentheses and *can* or *can't*.

1. Nick is a very good singer. (sing)   He can sing.
2. Mr. and Mrs. Lafitte are bad dancers. (dance)   _____
3. Trish is a bad artist. (draw)   _____
4. Doug is a great mechanic. (fix cars)   _____
5. Susan is a talented painter. (paint)   _____
6. Tran is a really bad cook. (cook)   _____

C Complete the conversation. Write *can* or *can't* and a verb from the box.

| bake | cook | dance | draw | paint | sing |

Antonio: What's your girlfriend like?

Hector: She's a great artist. She _____can draw_____ and she _____.
       1.   2.
Here are some of her pictures.

Antonio: Wow! They're beautiful.

Hector: Thanks. She's a great cook, too.

Antonio: Oh, yeah?

Hector: Yeah. She _____ Italian food! And she _____.
         3.   4.
She makes delicious chocolate cake.

Antonio: Wow! So, is she a good singer, too?

Hector: Oh, no. She _____. And she _____.
          5.   6.

Antonio: Too bad. You're a good dancer.

D CD 2 TRACK 47 Listen and check your answers.

TIME to TALK

WORK ALONE. Write a list of three people you know with talents.

PAIRS. Give your list to your partner. Student A, ask about one of the people on Student B's list. Student B, say one thing the person can and one thing the person can't do.

Example:
A: *What's Don like?*
B: *He's very talented. He can paint.*
   But he can't cook.

Don
Kevin
Doris

Vocabulary and Listening

Vocabulary

CD 2 TRACK 48 **Read and listen. Then listen and repeat.**

1. an airport
2. a daycare center
3. a hotel
4. an office
5. a factory
6. a pet shop
7. a nursery

PAIRS. **Student A, read a sentence. Student B, say where the people work. Make a sentence. There may be more than one correct answer.**

1. They help travelers.
2. They use machines.
3. They take care of plants.
4. They use computers.
5. They take care of children.
6. They take care of animals.

Example:
A: *They help travelers.*
B: *They work at a hotel.*
A: *Right.*

Listening

Two friends are talking.

A CD 2 TRACK **49** **Listen to the conversation. Answer the question.**

When can the woman work?

a. weekends

b. days

c. nights

B CD 2 TRACK **50** **Listen again. Write the missing word.**

Helen: I need a job. Do you have any ideas?

Eddie: What can you do?

Helen: Well, I can take care of children.

Eddie: Can you work during the day?

Helen: Yes, I can. I go to school in the evenings.

Eddie: Then maybe you can work in a _____ _____.

Helen: Good idea! But do I need a degree?

Eddie: I don't know. Good question! Ask the job counselor at your school.

Grammar to Communicate 2

CAN FOR ABILITY: *YES / NO* QUESTIONS

Can	Subject	Verb	Short Answers		
			Yes / No	Subject	Can / Can't
Can	I you he she Sue we they	help sick people? fix machines? take care of animals?	Yes,	you I he	can.
			No,	she we they	can't.

A Put the words in the correct order to make questions. Use capital letters as needed.

1. _Can you work in the evenings?_
   (work / in / you / can / evenings / the)

2. _____
   (Ms. Bonet / work / in / an / can / airport)

3. _____
   (can / plants / take care of / Gilberto)

4. _____
   (office / you / an / can / in / work)

5. _____
   (children / take care of / Chris / can)

B Complete the conversations. Use *can* or *can't*. Use capital letters as needed.

1. **A:** _____Can_____ you use office machines?

   B: Yes, I____can____. I use a computer and a copier at work.

2. **A:** _____ Ms. DaSilva fix cars?

   B: No, she _____. She's not good with cars.

3. **A:** _____ Mr. Yeoh work weekends?

   B: Yes, he _____. He has another job during the week.

4. **A:** _____ Fran take care of animals?

   B: No, she _____. She doesn't like them.

5. **A:** _____ you and Fred use computers?

   B: Yes, we _____. We work in a bank.

C 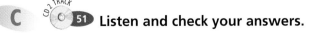 **51** **Listen and check your answers.**

                    See Pronunciation Activity B: page 211

CAN FOR ABILITY: INFORMATION QUESTIONS

Wh- Word	Can	Subject	Verb
What		you	do?
Where When	can	he Mr. Zack we	work? start?

D **Read the answers. Write questions. Use the words in parentheses. Add *can* and a verb.**

1. **A:** (When / Colin) _When can Colin work?_

   B: He can work on weekends.

2. **A:** (What / Mr. Simms) _____

   B: He can help sick people.

3. **A:** (When / Ted and Dave) _____

   B: They can start work on Monday.

4. **A:** (What / you) _____

   B: I can fix cars.

5. **A:** (Where / Randy) _____

   B: She can work in a pet shop.

WORK ALONE. Look at the questions in the chart. Write your answers in the column for Student A.

	STUDENT A	STUDENT B	STUDENT C
What can you do?			
Where can you work?			
When can you work?			

GROUPS OF 3. **Ask each other the questions. Write the answers.**

Example:
A: *What can you do?*
B: *I can help sick people.*
A: *Where can you work?*
B: *I can work in a hospital.*
A: *When can you work?*
B: *I can work nights.*

Reading and Writing

Reading

A Look at the job ads. What kind of information does each ad include?

1.
AUTO MECHANIC
7:30 A.M. – 3:30 P.M.
Monday – Friday
Call Monty **916-555-2095**

2.
Daycare worker
8:00 A.M.– 12:00 P.M.
Monday – Friday
Immediate openings
Apply within.

3.
SALESPERSON
9:30 A.M. – 2:30 P.M.
Saturday and Sunday
Apply online at
cooljobs.com.

4.
OFFICE WORKER
7:30 A.M. – 3:30 P.M.
Monday – Friday
Apply online at
cooljobs.com.

5.
HOSPITAL WORKER
4:00 P.M. – 12:00 A.M.
Saturday and Sunday
Immediate openings
Call 916-555-8035.

6.
SCHOOL BUS DRIVER
8:00 A.M. – 4:00 P.M.
Monday – Friday
Apply within.

B Read the sentences. What job in Exercise A can you do?

1. You can help sick people. _____#5_____

2. You can work weekends. _____ and _____

3. You can use a computer. _____

4. You can work mornings. _____

5. You can drive a bus. _____

6. You can fix cars. _____

7. You can take care of children. _____

8. You can work nights. _____

9. You can apply online. _____ and _____

10. You can apply by phone. _____ and _____

Prewriting

Look at the job application. Which job from page 178 is Melinda applying for?

Job Application

Melinda
First name

Grayson
Last name

L.
Middle initial

123 - 45 - 6789
Social Security Number

mgrayson@coolmail.com
E-mail address

23485 Robertson Blvd.   *2A*   *Los Angeles*   *CA*   *90242*   *510-555-3847*
Street Address   Apt.   City   State   ZIP   Phone Number

Position you are applying for: *Daycare worker*

Are you 18 or older? ✓ Yes ___ No   If not, what is your date of birth? _____

Are you legally authorized to work in the United States? ✓ Yes ___ No

Writing

Look at the ads on page 178. Choose one ad. Complete the application for that job. Use the application in Prewriting as a model.

Job Application

_____
First name

_____
Last name

_____
Middle initial

____-____-_____
Social Security Number

_____
E-mail address

_____   ____   _____   ____   ____   ____-____-____
Street Address   Apt.   City   State   ZIP   Phone Number

Position you are applying for: _____

Are you 18 or older? ___Yes ___ No   If not, what is your date of birth? _____

Are you legally authorized to work in the United States? ___ Yes ___ No

Put It in Place

Complete the charts with a verb from page 170.

AFFIRMATIVE STATEMENTS		
Subject	*Can*	Verb
I You He She We They	can	_____.

NEGATIVE STATEMENTS		
Subject	*Can*	Verb
I You He She We They	can't	_____.

YES / NO QUESTIONS		
Can	Subject	Verb
Can	you he she we they	_____?

INFORMATION QUESTIONS			
Wh- word	*Can*	Subject	Verb
Where	can	you he we	_____?

Put It Together: Can you . . . ?

PLAYERS	2 pairs of students
MATERIALS	1 book 1 coin (Heads = move 1 box. Tails = move 2 boxes) 2 markers (1 for each pair)
GOAL	To ask and answer questions about what you can do
EXAMPLE	Student A: Can you bake? Student B: Yes, I can. I can bake cakes and pies.
HOW TO PLAY	See page 221.

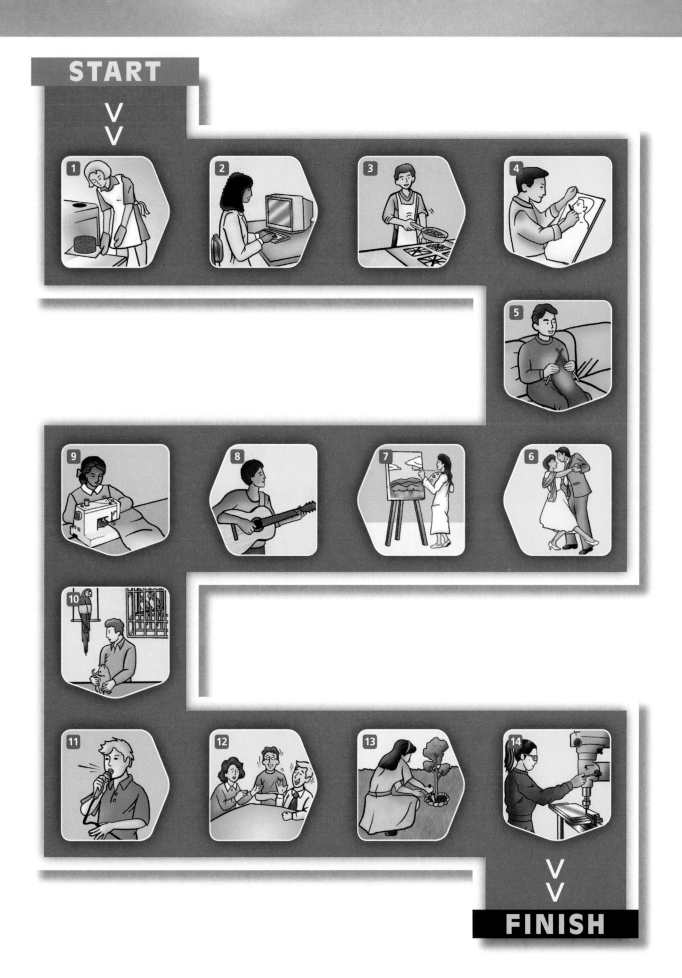

My boyfriend can't sing.

We were at home.

Grammar
- Simple Past of *Be*: Statements
- Simple Past of *Be*: Yes / No Questions and Short Answers
- Simple Past of *Be*: Wh- Questions

Vocabulary

CD 2 TRACK 52 Read and listen. Then listen and repeat.

PAIRS. Look at the pictures. What's your favorite place to be?

Example:

A: *My favorite place to be is at home. What about you?*

B: _____

CD 2 TRACK 53 Read and listen. Then listen and repeat.

PAIRS. Look at the calendar. Student A, say a time word or phrase, for example, "Last weekend." Student B, point to the word or phrase.

1. at home

2. at work

3. in school

4. at a wedding

5. at the mall

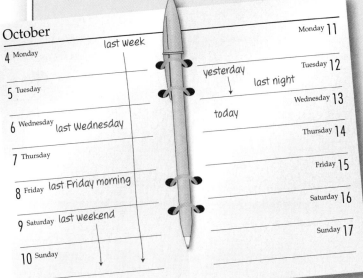

October

4 Monday	last week	Monday 11
5 Tuesday	yesterday last night	Tuesday 12
6 Wednesday last Wednesday	today	Wednesday 13
7 Thursday		Thursday 14
8 Friday last Friday morning		Friday 15
9 Saturday last weekend		Saturday 16
10 Sunday		Sunday 17

Listening

6. at the beach

7. at the movies

8. in the hospital

9. on vacation

10. on your honeymoon

A 🔘 **54 Listen to the conversation. Where was Charlotte last week? Check (✓) the correct picture.**

Pierre and Charlotte are co-workers.

B 🔘 **55 Listen again. Fill in the missing words.**

Pierre: Hi, Charlotte. Where were you _____ week? You weren't _____ work.

Charlotte: No, I was in Miami.

Pierre: Oh, yeah?

Charlotte: Yeah. I was _____ my cousin Gina's wedding _____ Saturday.

Pierre: How was the wedding?

Charlotte: Beautiful. The weather was great. Everyone was so happy.

Pierre: What about the party?

Charlotte: Oh, it was a lot of fun. About 50 people were there—family, friends, co-workers.

Pierre: *I* wasn't there.

Charlotte: Of course you weren't there. You don't know Gina!

We were at home.

Grammar to Communicate 1

Subject	*Was / Were*		Subject	*Was / Were*	*Not*		Contractions	
I He She It	was	in Miami.	I He She It	was	not	at work.	Was + not → Wasn't	
You We Sam and I They	were		You We They	were			Were + not → Weren't	

A Complete the sentences. Use *was* or *were*.

1. Hector _____ in San Francisco last week. His family _____ with him.

2. I _____ at home last night. It _____ cold outside!

3. Boris and Lana _____ not at work yesterday. They _____ in Miami.

4. We _____ at the movies last Sunday. The movie _____ great.

5. The weather _____ beautiful last weekend. We _____ at the beach.

6. Jae-Min _____ not in school last Tuesday. Her daughter _____ sick.

7. The wedding _____ in a park. It _____ beautiful.

8. Gus _____ not at home yesterday. He and his wife _____ at work.

B Rewrite each sentence. Use the time expression in parentheses.

1. Fung-Yee is at work. (yesterday)   *Fung-Yee was at work yesterday.*

2. Mustafa isn't at home. (last Sunday)   _____

3. She and her family aren't in Chile. (last year)   _____

4. I'm at the mall. (last night)   _____

5. You aren't in school. (yesterday)   _____

6. It's sunny and hot. (last week)   _____

7. Guy and his friends are at the beach.

   (last Saturday)   _____

C Look at the pictures and the words in parentheses. Write a sentence. Use contractions if possible.

1.

Harry wasn't at the beach last weekend.
(Harry / last weekend)

2.

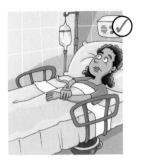

_____
(Cindy / last week)

3.

_____
(Mr. and Mrs. Ortiz / last night)

4.

_____
(Suzanne and Richard / last Saturday night)

5.

_____
(Reynaldo / last Friday)

6.

_____
(Ho / last Monday morning)

GROUPS. Tell your classmates about last weekend. Talk about the weather. Talk about where you were in the morning, afternoon, and night.

Example:

Last weekend, the weather was great. On Saturday morning, I was at home. On Saturday afternoon, I was at the mall. On Saturday night, I was at my friend's house. On Sunday morning, . . .

Report to the class. Were you and anyone in your group in the same place at the same time last weekend?

Example:

Lia and I were both at the mall on Saturday afternoon.

Vocabulary and Listening

Vocabulary

 56 **Read and listen. Then listen and repeat.**

JANUARY	FEBRUARY	MARCH	APRIL	MAY	JUNE
S M T W T F S	S M T W T F S	S M T W T F S	S M T W T F S	S M T W T F S	S M T W T F S
1 2 3 4 5 6 7	1 2 3 4	1 2 3 4	1	1 2 3 4 5 6	1 2 3
8 9 10 11 12 13 14	5 6 7 8 9 10 11	5 6 7 8 9 10 11	2 3 4 5 6 7 8	7 8 9 10 11 12 13	4 5 6 7 8 9 10
15 16 17 18 19 20 21	12 13 14 15 16 17 18	12 13 14 15 16 17 18	9 10 11 12 13 14 15	14 15 16 17 18 19 20	11 12 13 14 15 16 17
22 23 24 25 26 27 28	19 20 21 22 23 24 25	19 20 21 22 23 24 25	16 17 18 19 20 21 22	21 22 23 24 25 26 27	18 19 20 21 22 23 24
29 30 31	26 27 28	26 27 28 29 30 31	23 24 25 26 27 28 29 30	28 29 30 31	25 26 27 28 29 30

JULY	AUGUST	SEPTEMBER	OCTOBER	NOVEMBER	DECEMBER
S M T W T F S	S M T W T F S	S M T W T F S	S M T W T F S	S M T W T F S	S M T W T F S
1	1 2 3 4 5	1 2	1 2 3 4 5 6 7	1 2 3 4	1 2 3
2 3 4 5 6 7 8	6 7 8 9 10 11 12	3 4 5 6 7 8 9	8 9 10 11 12 13 14	5 6 7 8 9 10 11	4 5 6 7 8 9
9 10 11 12 13 14 15	13 14 15 16 17 18 19	10 11 12 13 14 15 16	15 16 17 18 19 20 21	12 13 14 15 16 17 18	10 11 12 13 14 15 16
16 17 18 19 20 21 22	20 21 22 23 24 25 26	17 18 19 20 21 22 23	22 23 24 25 26 27 28	19 20 21 22 23 24 25	17 18 19 20 21 22 23
23 24 25 26 27 28 29	27 28 29 30 31	24 25 26 27 28 29 30	29 30 31	26 27 28 29 30	24 25 26 27 28 29 30
30 31					31

PAIRS. **Talk about your favorite month.**

Example:

A: *What's your favorite month?*
B: *It's May. What's your favorite month?*
A: *It's _____.*

 57 **Read and listen. Then listen and repeat.**

the first	the ninth	the seventeenth	the twenty-fifth
the second	the tenth	the eighteenth	the twenty-sixth
the third	the eleventh	the nineteenth	the twenty-seventh
the fourth	the twelfth	the twentieth	the twenty-eighth
the fifth	the thirteenth	the twenty-first	the twenty-ninth
the sixth	the fourteenth	the twenty-second	the thirtieth
the seventh	the fifteenth	the twenty-third	the thirty-first
the eighth	the sixteenth	the twenty-fourth	

PAIRS. **Talk about birthdays and other important dates.**

Example:

A: *When is your birthday?*
B: *It's November 6. When is your birthday?*
A: *It's _____.*

Listening

CD 2 TRACK 58 **A** Listen to the conversation. Read the sentences. Check *True* or *False*.

Conversation Part 1	True	False
1. Liz was at work last week.	❏	❏
2. She was at Disney World.	❏	❏
3. Ramon was at Disney World last week.	❏	❏

Ramon and Liz are co-workers.

Conversation Part 2		
4. Ramon doesn't have children.	❏	❏
5. He was at Disney World with his wife.	❏	❏
6. He and his wife were married on June 4.	❏	❏

CD 2 TRACK 59 **B** Listen again. Write the missing dates.

Conversation Part 1

Ramon: Where were you last week?

Liz: I was on vacation—at Disney World.

Ramon: Disney World? I love Disney World. It's fantastic!

Liz: I know! When were *you* there?

Ramon: Last year. At the end of _____. We were there for ten days.

Liz: Were you there on _____?

Ramon: Yes! The fireworks were great!

Conversation Part 2

Liz: Who were you there with? You don't have kids.

Ramon: No. I was there with my wife. Just the two of us.

Liz: Really?

Ramon: Yeah. Why are you so surprised?

Liz: I don't know. People usually go there with their kids.

Ramon: Well, actually, we were on our honeymoon! It was very romantic.

Liz: Oh!

Ramon: Yup! We were married last _____.

Grammar to Communicate 2

SIMPLE PAST OF *BE*: YES / NO QUESTIONS AND SHORT ANSWERS

Was / Were	Subject					Short Answers				
				Yes	Subject	Was / Were	No	Subject	Wasn't / Weren't
Was	I he she Tom	at Disney World last year?		Yes,	you	were.	No,	you	weren't.
					he she I	was.		he she I	wasn't.
Were	you we they				we they	were.		we they	weren't.

A Write questions. Use the words in parentheses. Then look at Enrique's daily planner. Answer the question. Give a short answer and write another sentence.

1. **A:** Was Enrique in Mexico City on March 31?
   (Enrique / in Mexico City / on March 31)

   B: No, he wasn't. He was in New York.

   MARCH
   Monday   30
   Tuesday New York 31

2. **A:** _____
   (Enrique and his family / at home / on August 19)

   B: _____

   AUGUST
   Friday   18
   Saturday   19
   family vacation in Canada

3. **A:** _____
   (Enrique's children / in school / on September 1)

   B: _____

   SEPTEMBER
   Monday   6
   Tuesday (school starts) 7

4. **A:** _____
   (Enrique / at work / on November 24)

   B: _____

   NOVEMBER
   Wednesday   23
   Thursday   24
   Holiday—Thanksgiving

See Pronunciation Activity B: page 212

SIMPLE PAST OF *BE*: *WH-* QUESTIONS

Wh- Word	*Was / Were*	Subject		
Where	was	I he she it	in July?	In Disney World.
How			?	Great!
When	were	you we they	in Disney World?	In July.
Who			with?	John and Ellie.

Wh- Questions About the Subject				
Wh- Word	*Was / Were*	Subject		
Who	was		in Miami?	My brother.

B Read the answers. Complete the questions. Use *Who*, *Where*, *When*, and *How*.

1. **A:** ___Where___ were you on New Year's Eve?

   B: I was at a restaurant in the city.

   A: _____ were you there with?

   B: My wife and some friends.

2. **A:** _____ were you on vacation?

   B: In June. We were in San Diego.

   A: _____ was the weather?

   B: It was great. It was sunny and warm.

C **60** **Listen and check your answers.**

PAIRS. **Practice the conversations in Exercise B.**

PAIRS. **Repeat the conversations in Exercise B, but now give true answers.**

Example:
A: *Where were you on New Year's Eve?*
B: *I was at a party at my friend's house.*

We were at home. (189)

Reading and Writing

Reading

A **Look at the list of U.S. bank holidays for 2006.**

County Bank
Holidays 2006

New Year's Day 2006	Monday, January 2, 2006*
Martin Luther King, Jr. Day	Monday, January 16, 2006
Presidents' Day	Monday, February 20, 2006
Memorial Day	Monday, May 29, 2006
Independence Day	Tuesday, July 4, 2006
Labor Day	Monday, September 4, 2006
Columbus Day	Monday, October 9, 2006
Veterans' Day	Saturday, November 11, 2006
Thanksgiving Day	Thursday, November 23, 2006
Christmas Day	Monday, December 25, 2006

B **Answer the questions about the 2006 bank holidays.**

1. What holiday was on 9/4/2006? <u>Labor Day.</u>

2. What holiday was on 2/20/2006? _____

3. What holiday was on 5/29/06? _____

4. What holiday was on 11/11/06? _____

5. What holiday was on 1/16/06? _____

6. What holiday was on 12-25-06? _____

7. What holiday was on 11-23-06? _____

8. What day was 10-9-06? _____

9. What holiday was on 1-2-06? _____

10. What holiday was on 7-4-06? _____

*Sunday holidays are celebrated on Mondays.

Prewriting

Rewrite the dates. Use the abbreviations in the box.

January → Jan.	May	September → Sept.
February → Feb.	June	October → Oct.
March → Mar.	July	November → Nov.
April → Apr.	August → Aug.	December → Dec.

Other 2006 Holidays

1. Groundhog Day
   2/2/06: _Feb. 2, 2006_

2. Valentine's Day
   2/14/06: _____

3. St. Patrick's Day
   3/17/06: _____

4. Mother's Day
   5/14/06: _____

5. Father's Day
   6/18/06: _____

6. Halloween
   10/31/06: _____

7. Election Day
   11/7/06: _____

Writing

Write the following dates. Write them three ways.

1. Today's date.
   March 10, 2007   _3/10/07_   _Mar. 10, 2007_

2. Your date of birth.
   _____ _____ _____

3. Another important date in your life.
   _____ _____ _____

   Why is this date important to you?
   _____

Review

Put It in Place

Complete the charts with *was*, *wasn't*, *were*, and *weren't*. Use capital letters as needed.

SIMPLE PAST OF *BE*: *YES* / *NO* QUESTIONS

Affirmative Short Answers				Subject	Was / Were		Subject	Wasn't / Weren't
Was / Were	**Subject**							
_____	I	at home yesterday?	Yes,	you	_____.	No,	you	_____.
	he			he	_____.		he	_____.
_____	they			they	_____.		they	_____.

SIMPLE PAST OF *BE*: *WH*- QUESTIONS

Wh- Word	Was / Were	Subject	
Where	_____	she it	on Valentine's Day?
How			?
When	_____	you we	in San Francisco?
Who			with?

WH- QUESTIONS ABOUT THE SUBJECT

Wh- Word	Was / Were	
Who	_____	at work?

Put It Together: Where were you?

PLAYERS	2 pairs of students
MATERIALS	1 book 1 coin (Heads = move 1 box. Tails = move 2 boxes) 2 markers (1 for each pair)
GOAL	To ask and answer questions using the simple past
EXAMPLE	Student A: Who was married on May 2? Student B: Nina and Gerald.
HOW TO PLAY	See page 221.

START

FINISH

Who / married / on May 2?

Yes / No? Albert / at work / on 7/15?

Where / Diane and Neil / on 3/10?

When / Nina and Gerald's wedding?

Who / the surprise party for?

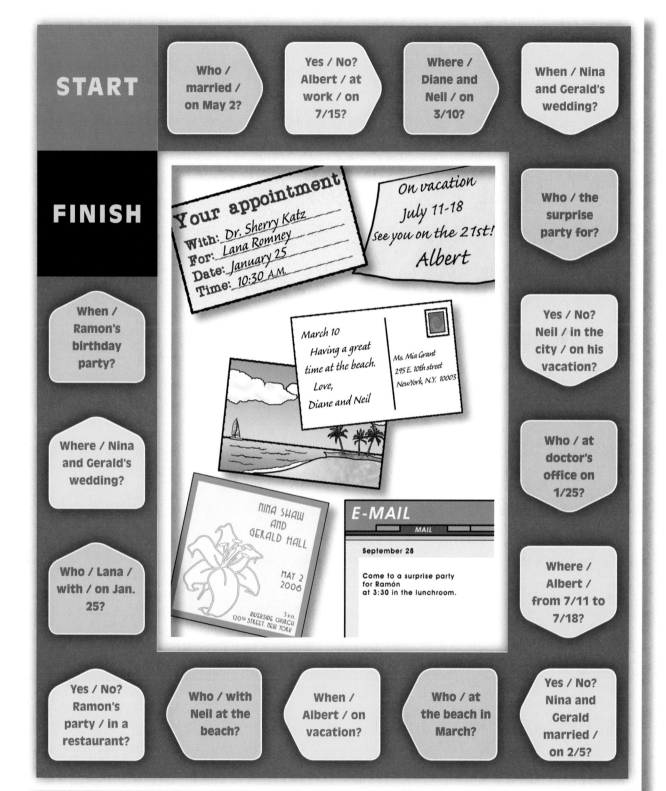

Your appointment
With: Dr. Sherry Katz
For: Lana Romney
Date: January 25
Time: 10:30 A.M.

On vacation July 11-18
See you on the 21st!
Albert

March 10
Having a great time at the beach.
Love,
Diane and Neil

Ms. Mia Grant
295 E. 10th street
New York, N.Y. 10003

NINA SHAW AND GERALD HALL
MAY 2 2006
5 p.m.
RIVERSIDE CHURCH
120TH STREET, NEW YORK

E-MAIL
MAIL
September 28
Come to a surprise party for Ramón at 3:30 in the lunchroom.

When / Ramon's birthday party?

Where / Nina and Gerald's wedding?

Who / Lana / with / on Jan. 25?

Yes / No? Ramon's party / in a restaurant?

Who / with Neil at the beach?

When / Albert / on vacation?

Who / at the beach in March?

Yes / No? Nina and Gerald married / on 2/5?

Where / Albert / from 7/11 to 7/18?

Where / Albert / from 7/11 to 7/18?

Who / at doctor's office on 1/25?

Yes / No? Neil / in the city / on his vacation?

World Map

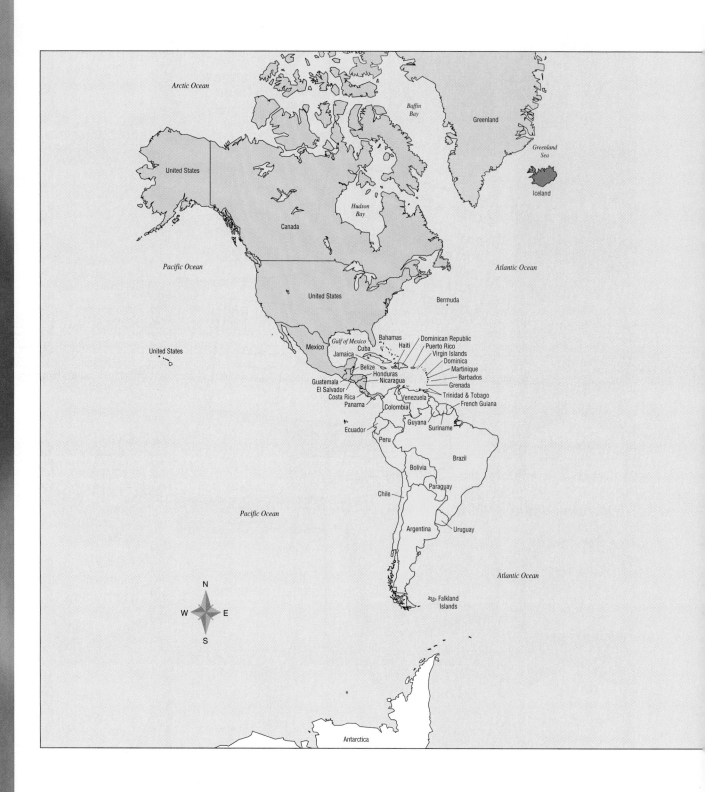

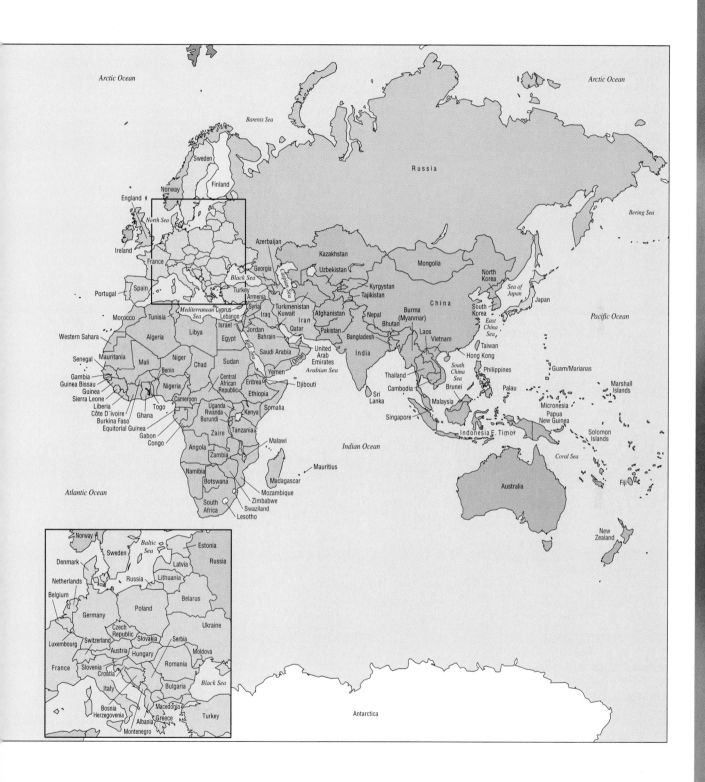

Arctic Ocean

Barents Sea

Arctic Ocean

Bering Sea

Sweden

Russia

Norway

England

North Sea

Finland

Ireland

Azerbaijan

Kazakhstan

Mongolia

North Korea

Sea of Japan

France

Georgia

Uzbekistan

Black Sea

Caspian Sea

Kyrgystan

China

South Korea

Japan

Pacific Ocean

Portugal

Spain

Turkey

Armenia

Tajikistan

Mediterranean Sea

Cyprus

Syria

Turkmenistan

Afghanistan

Nepal

Burma (Myanmar)

East China Sea

Morocco

Tunisia

Lebanon

Iraq

Kuwait

Iran

Bhutan

Laos

Taiwan

Israel

Jordan

Qatar

Pakistan

Bangladesh

Vietnam

Hong Kong

Western Sahara

Algeria

Libya

Egypt

Bahrain

India

Saudi Arabia

Oman

United Arab Emirates

South China Sea

Philippines

Guam/Marianas

Senegal

Mauritania

Mali

Niger

Chad

Sudan

Yemen

Arabian Sea

Djibouti

Thailand

Brunei

Palau

Marshall Islands

Gambia

Benin

Eritrea

Cambodia

Guinea Bissau

Guinea

Nigeria

Central African Republic

Ethiopia

Sri Lanka

Malaysia

Micronesia

Sierra Leone

Cameroon

Singapore

Papua New Guinea

Liberia

Uganda

Rwanda

Kenya

Somalia

Solomon Islands

Côte D´ivoire

Ghana

Togo

Burundi

Indonesia

E. Timor

Burkina Faso

Tanzania

Equitorial Guinea

Gabon

Congo

Zaire

Malawi

Indian Ocean

Coral Sea

Angola

Zambia

Mauritius

Namibia

Botswana

Madagascar

Australia

Fiji

Atlantic Ocean

Mozambique

Zimbabwe

South Africa

Swaziland

Lesotho

New Zealand

Norway

Baltic Sea

Estonia

Denmark

Sweden

Latvia

Russia

Netherlands

Russia

Lithuania

Belgium

Poland

Belarus

Germany

Czech Republic

Ukraine

Luxembourg

Switzerland

Slovakia

Serbia

France

Austria

Hungary

Moldova

Slovenia

Croatia

Romania

Italy

Bulgaria

Black Sea

Bosnia Herzegovina

Macedonia

Albania

Greece

Turkey

Montenegro

Antarctica

United States and Canada Map

Pronunciation Activities

Unit 1

A. The pronunciation of *I'm*, *is*, and *it's*

1. 🔘 **2** Listen. Notice the weak pronunciation of *I'm*, *is*, and *it's* in these sentences.

   I'm Fred Black.

   My name is Carina.

   It's nice to meet you.

2. **Write *I'm*, *is*, or *it's*.**

   a. _____ nice to meet you, too.

   b. _____ Pat Logan.

   c. My name _____ Robin North.

3. 🔘 **3** Listen and check your answers. Then listen and repeat.

B. The sound /h/ in *he's* and /ʃ/ in *she's*

1. 🔘 **4** Listen. Notice the sound /h/ in *he's* and /ʃ/ in *she's*.

   He's my teacher.

   She's my friend.

2. 🔘 **5** Listen. Write *He's* or *She's*.

   a. _____ my classmate.

   b. _____ nice.

   c. _____ the teacher.

   d. _____ cute.

   e. _____ my friend.

   PAIRS. **Check your answers.**

3. 🔘 **6** Listen again and repeat.

Unit 2

A. Stress in words

1. **[CD 3 TRACK 7]** Some words, like *Spain*, have one syllable. Some words, like *Peru*, have two syllables: Pe·ru. Some words, like *Korea*, have three syllables: Ko·re·a. When words have more than one syllable, one syllable is loud and strong. It is stressed. Notice the stressed syllable in the names of the countries:

Chi na   Pe ru   Ger ma ny   Ko re a

_____   _____   _____   _____

_____   _____   _____

_____   _____   _____

2. **[CD 3 TRACK 8]** Listen. Write the names of these countries in the correct column above.

Brazil	England	Italy	Mexico	Somalia
Canada	Ireland	Japan	Russia	Taiwan

PAIRS. Check your answers.

3. **[CD 3 TRACK 9]** Listen again and repeat.

B. Intonation in questions and statements

1. **[CD 3 TRACK 10]** Listen. Notice that the voice jumps up and then falls at the end of statements. Notice that the voice goes up at the end of *yes/no* questions.

Are you British? ↗

Yes, I am. ↘ I'm from England. ↘

2. **[CD 3 TRACK 11]** Listen. Draw an arrow to show that the voice goes up or down.

a. Is he from Mexico?

b. Yes, he is.

c. Is your friend Korean?

d. No, she isn't. She's Chinese.

PAIRS. Check your answers.

3. **[CD 3 TRACK 12]** Listen again and repeat.

Unit 3

A. The pronunciation of *a* and *an*

1. 🔘 **13** *A* and *an* are usually weak, or unstressed. Notice the weak pronunciation of *a* /ə/ and *an* /ən/.

    a mechanic

    an actor

2. **Write *a* or *an*.**

    a. _____ homemaker

    b. _____ artist

    c. _____ engineer

    d. _____ painter

    e. _____ doctor

3. 🔘 **14** **Listen and check your answers. Then listen and repeat.**

B. Weak form of *be*

1. 🔘 **15** The forms of *be* (*am*, *is*, *are*) are often weak, or unstressed. We usually use contractions, like *I'm* and *he's*, in speaking. Notice the pronunciation of *is* and *are* and the contraction *he's* in these sentences.

    Your children **are** cute.

    How old **is** your son?

    He's twelve.

2. 🔘 **16** **Listen. Write the missing words.**

    a. Where __are__ your children?

    b. _____ in Dallas, with my parents.

    c. How old _____ they?

    d. My son _____ ten.

    e. My daughter _____ seven.

    f. _____ great kids.

    PAIRS. **Check your answers.**

3. 🔘 **17** **Listen again and repeat.**

Unit 4

A. The pronunciation of *your*, *our*, and *their*

1. **18** **Listen. Notice the weak pronunciation of *your*, *our*, and *their*.**

   What's your phone number?

   He's our friend.

   What are their names?

2. **19** **Listen. Write *your*, *our*, or *their*.**

   a. _____ teacher is great.

   b. _____ son is cute.

   c. What's _____ phone number?

   d. What's _____ address?

   e. _____ children are in high school.

   f. Here's _____ e-mail address.

   PAIRS. **Check your answers.**

3. **20** **Listen again and repeat.**

B. The pronunciation of possessive *-s*

1. **21** **Listen. Notice the three pronunciations of the possessive –s ending.**

/s/	/z/	/ɪz/
Jack's	Sally's	Dennis's
Pat's	Tim's	Liz's

2. **22** **Listen. Write these possessives in the correct column.**

Alice's	Collette's	Mary's	Ming's	Rick's	Rose's

/s/	/z/	/ɪz/
_____	_____	_____
_____	_____	_____

   PAIRS. **Check your answers.**

3. **23** **Listen again and repeat.**

Unit 5

A. The pronunciation of the plural -s ending

1. 🔘 **24** **Listen. Notice the three pronunciations of the plural -s ending.**

/s/	/z/	/ɪz/
book**s**	dictionarie**s**	bookcase**s**

2. 🔘 **25** **Listen. Write these plurals in the correct column.**

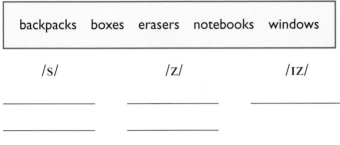

backpacks   boxes   erasers   notebooks   windows

/s/	/z/	/ɪz/
_____	_____	_____
_____	_____	

PAIRS. **Check your answers.**

3. 🔘 **26** **Listen again and repeat.**

B. Weak words in sentences

1. 🔘 **27** *A*, *the*, *and*, *to*, and *your* are usually weak, or unstressed, in sentences. **Listen. Notice the weak pronunciation of these words.**

Don't use a pen.

Close the window, please.

Listen and repeat.

Go to the board.

Open your workbooks.

2. 🔘 **28** **Listen. Write the missing words.**

   a. Please erase _____ board.

   b. Turn _____ page 23.

   c. Copy _____ words in _____ notebooks.

   d. Take out _____ pencil _____ an eraser.

   PAIRS. **Check your answers.**

3. 🔘 **29** **Listen again and repeat.**

Unit 6

A. The vowel sound /ə/

1. [CD 3 TRACK 30] **Listen. Notice the weak pronunciation of the vowels in blue in these words. They have the sound /ə/.**

an**o**ther

t**o**day

2. [CD 3 TRACK 31] **Listen. Write the missing letters.**

   a. d____grees

   b. ____gain

   c. list____n

   d. favor____te

   e. temper____ture

   PAIRS. **Check your answers.**

3. [CD 3 TRACK 32] **Listen again and repeat.**

B. Linking

1. [CD 3 TRACK 33] **Listen. Notice that we link a consonant sound (like *m*, *z*, or *t*) at the end of a word to a vowel sound (like *a*, *u*, *i*, or /ə/) at the beginning of the next word.**

   What time is it?

   When are your classes?

2. [CD 3 TRACK 34] **Listen. Draw lines to show the linking.**

   a. When is your class?

   b. My class is at six.

   c. It's on Tuesday.

   d. What time is the test?

   e. It's at eight o'clock.

   PAIRS. **Check your answers.**

3. [CD 3 TRACK 35] **Listen again and repeat.**

Unit 7

A. The pronunciation of *th*

1. **CD 3 TRACK 36** Listen. Notice the pronunciation of *th* in *this*, *that*, *these*, and *those*. To form the /ð/ sound, put your tongue between your teeth.

   this skirt

   those shoes

2. **CD 3 TRACK 37** Listen. Write *this*, *that*, *these*, or *those*.

   a. _____ blouse   e. _____ socks

   b. _____ sneakers   f. _____ jeans

   c. _____ shirt   g. _____ T-shirt

   d. _____ pants   h. _____ suit

   PAIRS. **Check your answers.**

3. **CD 3 TRACK 38** Listen again and repeat.

B. The pronunciation of prices

1. **CD 3 TRACK 39** Listen. Notice the way we say prices.

   It's 99¢.

   It's $1.25.

   It's $7.03.

   It's $15.99.

   It's $15.00.

   It's $350.00.

2. Write the words for these prices.

   a. $12.85   _____

   b. $47.00   _____

   c. $63.97   _____

   d. $10.75   _____

   e. $1.89   _____

   f. $225.00   _____

3. **CD 3 TRACK 40** Listen and check your answers. Then listen and repeat.

Unit 8

A. The pronunciation of *there's* and *there are*

1. 🔘 **41** **Listen. Notice the pronunciation of *there's* and *there are*. For *there is*, we contract *there* and *is* to make *there's*. For *there are*, we reduce *are* to /ə/.**

   There's a dining room.

   There are three bedrooms.

2. **Write *There's* or *There are*.**

   a. _____ carpeting in the bedroom.

   b. _____ no dining room.

   c. _____ blinds on the windows.

   d. _____ a big kitchen.

   e. _____ two bathrooms.

3. 🔘 **42** **Listen and check your answers. Then listen and repeat.**

B. Stress in words

1. 🔘 **43** **Listen. Notice the pronunciation. One syllable is stressed. It is louder and longer.**

   •
   kitchen

   •
   apartment

2. **Underline the stressed syllable.**

   a. car pet ing

   b. clos et

   c. dish wash er

   d. dry er

   e. re frig er a tor

   f. mi cro wave

3. 🔘 **44** **Listen and check your answers. Then listen and repeat.**

Unit 9

A. Stress used to contrast information

1. 🔊 **45** **Listen. Notice that we stress the words in contrast.**

   Natasha likes **hot dogs**, but her brothers like **hamburgers**.

   I want a **tuna** sandwich, but my husband wants a **turkey** sandwich.

2. 🔊 **46** **Listen. Fill in the missing words.**

   a. Ms. Rios likes _____, but her husband likes _____.

   b. Nabil wants a grilled _____ sandwich, but Dan wants a grilled _____ sandwich.

   c. My son likes _____, but my daughter likes _____.

   PAIRS. **Check your answers.**

3. 🔊 **47** **Listen again and repeat.**

B. The pronunciation of *don't* and *doesn't*

1. 🔊 **48** **Listen. Notice the pronunciation of the contractions *don't* and *doesn't*.**

   I **don't** like chicken.

   It **doesn't** need sugar.

2. **Write *don't* or *doesn't*.**

   a. The baby _____ want juice now.

   b. We _____ like soda.

   c. Mr. and Mrs. Song _____ need milk for their coffee.

   d. Will _____ want dessert.

   e. The soup _____ need salt.

   f. Eleni _____ like chocolate.

3. 🔊 **49** **Listen and check your answers. Then listen and repeat.**

Unit 10

A. The pronunciation of *has* and *have*

1. 🔊 **50** **Listen. Notice the pronunciation of /v/ in *have* and /z/ in *has*.**

   I **have** a cold.

   Maurice **has** a sore throat.

2. **Write *have* or *has*.**

   a. My daughter _____ a fever.

   b. We _____ the flu.

   c. Ms. Sayed _____ a cough.

   d. Misha _____ a backache.

   e. I _____ a cold.

   f. Mr. Ito _____ a stomachache.

3. 🔊 **51** **Listen and check your answers. Then listen and repeat.**

B. Weak form of *do*

1. 🔊 **52** **Listen. Notice the short, weak pronunciation of *do* in these questions. The word *do* sounds like *d'*.**

   Do you feel tired?

   Do we want a doctor?

   Do they need medicine?

2. 🔊 **53** **Listen. Write *Do you*, *Do we*, or *Do they*.**

   a. _____ have aspirin?

   b. _____ need cough medicine?

   c. _____ want water?

   d. _____ feel better now?

   e. _____ have a sore throat?

   f. _____ want chicken soup?

   PAIRS. **Check your answers.**

3. 🔊 **54** **Listen again and repeat.**

Unit 11

A. Sentence rhythm

1. 🎵 CD 3 TRACK **55** Listen. Notice the rhythm in sentences. Important words are stressed. They are long and loud.

I **always** check **e-mail** at **night**.

He **sometimes** cooks **dinner**.

They **never get** up **early**.

2. 🎵 CD 3 TRACK **56** Listen. Underline the stressed words.

   a. The <u>children</u> <u>never</u> do the <u>dishes</u>.

   b. I brush my teeth every morning.

   c. We go to bed late.

   d. He takes a shower after work.

   e. She gets home early on Friday.

   PAIRS. **Check your answers.**

3. 🎵 CD 3 TRACK **57** Listen again and repeat.

B. Linking in *does he* and *does she*

1. 🎵 CD 3 TRACK **58** Listen. In questions, *does* has a weak pronunciation. Notice how we link *does* to *he* ("duzzee"). Notice how we link *does* to *she* ("dushee").

Where **does he** play cards?

When **does she** go dancing?

2. 🎵 CD 3 TRACK **59** Listen. Write *does he* or *does she*.

   a. How often _____ visit you?

   b. What time _____ play soccer?

   c. When _____ relax?

   d. Where _____ eat out?

   e. How often _____ get a DVD?

   f. When _____ watch TV?

   PAIRS. **Check your answers.**

3. 🎵 CD 3 TRACK **60** Listen again and repeat.

Unit 12

A. Stress in compound nouns

1. 🔊 **61** Some nouns are made up of two words, like *coffee shop*. They are called compound nouns. Notice that the first word in compound nouns is stressed.

   coffee shop

   movie theater

2. 🔊 **62** Listen. Underline the stressed word in the compound nouns in each sentence.

   a. The <u>post</u> office is next to the bank.

   b. The gas station is on the corner.

   c. The police station is across from the park.

   d. The coffee shop is next to the drugstore.

   e. The restaurant is across from the department store.

   f. The parking lot is next to the hospital.

   PAIRS. Check your answers.

3. 🔊 **63** Listen again and repeat.

B. Weak pronunciation of *it* and *them*

1. 🔊 **64** Listen. Notice the weak pronunciation of the object pronouns *it* and *them*. They are unstressed.

   We get **it** at Shop 'N Shop.

   I cook **them** in the microwave.

2. **Write *it* or *them*.**

   a. My kids like cookies. I buy _____ every week.

   b. Can you get milk? We need _____ for our coffee.

   c. We eat a lot of ice cream. We have _____ for dessert.

   d. Eggs are sometimes expensive. I buy _____ on sale.

   e. Do you like salad? I eat _____ every day.

3. 🔊 **65** Listen and check your answers. Then listen and repeat.

Unit 13

A. The pronunciation of the sounds /m/, /n/, and /ŋ/ at the end of words

1. **66** Listen. Notice that we pronounce the sounds /m/, /n/, and /ŋ/ clearly at the end of a word.

   mo**m**

   liste**n**

   study**ing**

2. **67** Listen. Write the missing words.

   a. They're _____ e-mail.

   b. What do you do in your free _____?

   c. He's _____ on his cell _____.

   d. She's _____ in the _____.

   e. We're _____ TV in the _____ _____.

   PAIRS. **Check your answers.**

3. **68** Listen again and repeat.

B. The pronunciation of *isn't* and *aren't*

1. **69** Listen. Notice the pronunciation of the contractions *isn't* and *aren't*.

   Kenny **isn't** doing his homework.

   We **aren't** cleaning the house.

2. **Write *isn't* or *aren't*.**

   a. Mr. Soto _____ getting the mail.

   b. Kyung _____ taking out the trash.

   c. Noemi and Keiko _____ checking e-mail.

   d. My mother and I _____ doing the laundry.

   e. Bernie _____ fixing the window.

   f. You _____ helping!

3. **70** Listen and check your answers. Listen again and repeat.

Unit 14

A. The pronunciation of *am*, *is(n't)*, and *are(n't)* at the end of a sentence

1. 🔘 **71** **Listen. Notice that we use a strong pronunciation of *am*, *is*, *isn't*, *are*, and *aren't* when they are at the end of a sentence.**

   Yes, I **am**.

   Yes, he **is**.

   No, he **isn't**.

   Yes, they **are**.

   No, they **aren't**.

2. **Complete the sentences.**

   a. Is Monica taking the subway? Yes, she _____.

   b. Is Jerry riding his bike? No, he _____.

   c. Are your parents taking a taxi? Yes, they _____.

   d. Are you on your way home? No, we _____.

   e. Are you driving now? Yes, I _____.

3. 🔘 **72** **Listen and check your answers. Then listen and repeat.**

B. Weak pronunciation of *are*

1. 🔘 **73** **Listen. Notice the weak pronunciation of *are* in these questions.**

   When **are** you going?

   Where **are** they walking?

2. 🔘 **74** **Listen. Write the missing words.**

   a. _____ they doing?

   b. _____ we waiting for?

   c. _____ you turning?

   d. _____ they going to work?

   e. _____ you talking to?

   f. _____ you parking?

   PAIRS. **Check your answers.**

3. 🔘 **75** **Listen again and repeat.**

Unit 15

A. The pronunciation of *can* and *can't* before a verb

1. 🔘 **76** **Listen. Notice the pronunciation of *can* and *can't* before a verb. *Can* is unstressed and has a weak pronunciation. *Can't* is stressed and has a strong pronunciation.**

He **can** sing.

He **can't** dance.

2. 🔘 **77** **Listen. Write *can* or *can't*.**

   a. Joe _____ play the piano.

   b. I _____ sew.

   c. His children _____ cook.

   d. Rick _____ tell jokes.

   e. My mother _____ knit.

   f. Sue _____ bake cakes.

   PAIRS. **Check your answers.**

3. 🔘 **78** **Listen again and repeat.**

B. The pronunciation of *can* and *can't* in short answers

1. 🔘 **79** **Listen. Notice the pronunciation of *can* and *can't* in short answers. They are stressed and have a strong pronunciation.**

Can you sing? Yes, I **can**.

Can they dance? No, they **can't**.

2. **Complete the sentences.**

   a. Can you paint? Yes, _____.

   b. Can he cook? No, _____.

   c. Can they draw? Yes, _____.

   d. Can she play the guitar? Yes, _____.

   e. Can you dance? No, _____.

3. 🔘 **80** **Listen and check your answers. Then listen and repeat.**

Unit 16

A. The pronunciation of *was*, *were*, *wasn't*, and *weren't* in statements

1. 🔊 **81** Listen. Notice the pronunciation of *was*, *were*, *wasn't*, and *weren't*. *Was* and *were* are unstressed and have weak pronunciations. *Wasn't* and *weren't* are stressed and have strong pronunciations.

   I **was** in L.A. last week.

   They **were** at home last night.

   He **wasn't** in school yesterday.

   We **weren't** there on Monday.

2. 🔊 **82** Listen. Write *was*, *were*, *wasn't*, or *weren't*.

   a. Dalia _____ in school last night.

   b. Ling and I _____ at the mall yesterday.

   c. Mr. and Mrs. Oh _____ in the park on Sunday.

   d. Tomiko _____ at home last Friday night.

   e. They _____ at the beach on Saturday.

   f. The wedding _____ beautiful.

   PAIRS. **Check your answers.**

3. 🔊 **83** Listen again and repeat.

B. Linking in *was he* and *was she*

1. 🔊 **84** In questions, *was* has a weak pronunciation. Listen. Notice how we link *was* to *he* ("wuzzee"). Notice how we link *was* to *she* ("wushee").

   Was he in Dallas?   Was she at home?

2. 🔊 **85** Listen. Write *Was he* or *Was she*.

   a. _____ at work yesterday?

   b. _____ there in March?

   c. _____ in Lima last year?

   d. _____ in the U.S. in 2006?

   e. _____ on vacation last week?

   f. _____ with you in Orlando?

   PAIRS. **Check your answers.**

3. 🔊 **86** Listen again and repeat.

Spelling Rules

Spelling Rules: Plural Nouns

1. To form the plural of most nouns, add –s.	one book ⟶ two books a pen ⟶ five pens
2. To form the plural of nouns that end in –ch, –s, –sh, –ss, –x, or –z, add –es.	one box ⟶ two boxes a glass ⟶ ten glasses
3. To form the plural of nouns that end in a consonant + –y, change the –y to –i and add –es.	one dictionary ⟶ two dictionaries a battery ⟶ four batteries

Spelling Rules: Third Person Singular Simple Present Verbs

1. To form the third person singular simple present of most verbs, add –s.	I like ⟶ he likes we need ⟶ she needs
2. To form the third person singular simple present of verbs that end in –ch, –s, –sh, –ss, –x, or –z, add –es.	I watch ⟶ he watches we brush ⟶ she brushes
3. To form the third person singular simple present of verbs that end in a consonant + –y, change the –y to –i and add –es.	I carry ⟶ he carries we study ⟶ she studies

Spelling Rules: -ing Form of the Verb

1. To form the –ing form of most verbs, add –ing to the base form of the verb.	read ⟶ reading listen ⟶ listening
2. To form the –ing form of verbs that end in –e, drop the –e and add –ing to the base form of the verb.	live ⟶ living write ⟶ writing
3. To form the –ing form of one-syllable verbs that consist of a consonant + vowel + consonant, double the final consonant and add –ing to the base form of the verb.	get ⟶ getting run ⟶ running

Capitalization and Punctuation Rules

Capitalization Rules

1. Capitalize the personal pronoun *I*.	My mother and **I** live in Florida.
2. Capitalize the first letter of the names of specific people and places.	**D**avid **W**illiams **T**oronto, **C**anada
3. Capitalize the first letter of titles.	**M**r. Keaton **M**s. Press
4. Capitalize the first letter of days and months.	**S**unday **J**anuary
5. Capitalize the first letter of nationalities and languages.	**B**razilian **E**nglish
6. Capitalize the first letter of the first word of a sentence.	**H**ow are you? **W**e like chocolate cake.

Punctuation Rules

1. Use a period at the end of a sentence.	I go to school in the evening**.** Please close the door**.**
2. Use a question mark at the end of a question.	What time is it**?** Do you drive to school**?**
3. Use an apostrophe in contractions.	She's a teacher. They don't work on the weekend.
4. Use an apostrophe to show possession with nouns.	My sister's name is Ana. Marc's phone number is 914-555-8938.

How to Play the Games

Unit 1: Spelling, PAGE 13

▶ You each have pictures of famous people together with their names. Cover your partner's side of the page.

▶ Student A: Look at the pictures and the names. Give and spell the names on your list.

▶ Student B: Write the names.

▶ Take turns.

Example
A: Person 1. His first name is Jamie.
B: Could you spell that, please?
A: J-A-M-I-E.
B: J-A-M-I-E?
A: Right. His last name is Foxx.
B: Could you spell that, please?
A: F-O-X-X.
B: F-O-X-X?
A: Right.
B: Person 5. Her first name is _____.

Unit 2: Around the World, PAGE 25

▶ Put your markers on the START box. Pair A goes first.

▶ Pair A: Toss the coin. Move one or two boxes. Read the words below the picture. Make a conversation.

Example
Penelope Cruz / from Mexico?
Student A: Is Penelope Cruz from Mexico?
Student B: No, she isn't. She's from Spain.

▶ All the information is in the unit! Try to remember. You can look back if you need to.

▶ Pair B: Make sure the conversation is correct. If the conversation is *not* correct, Pair A's marker goes back to the box from their last turn.

▶ Pair B: Take your turn.

▶ If you land on the box that has the other pair's marker, move to the next box.

▶ Continue to take turns. The first pair to get to the FINISH box wins.

▶ Try to get four boxes in a row, across ➡, down ↓, or diagonal ↘.

▶ Take turns. Student A goes first. Choose a box. Look at the picture and make a sentence. Student B, make sure the sentence is correct.

▶ If the sentence is correct, write A (for Student A) or B (for Student B) in the box. You cannot choose a box with a letter already in it.

Example
Student A: Number 1. She's a lawyer.
Student B: Right. (*Student A writes "A."*) My turn. Number _____.

▶ The first student to get four boxes in a row wins.

▶ You each have forms for the same people, but the information is not complete. Cover your partner's side of the page.

▶ Student A: Look at your forms. Ask Student B for the missing information (in yellow). Write the information.

▶ Student B: Ask Student A.

Example
A: What's Brad Smith's address?
B: It's 18376 Shore Drive.
A: 18376 Shore Drive?
B: Right. What's his ZIP code?
A: It's 91074.
B: Could you repeat that, please?

▶ Take turns.

Student A's Information

EMERGENCY CONTACT FORM

Name:
Brad Smith

Address:
Los Angeles, CA 91074

Phone No.:

E-mail Address:
bradsmith@coolmail.com

Student B's Information

EMERGENCY CONTACT FORM

Name:
Brad Smith

Address:
18376 Shore Drive
Los Angeles, CA

Phone No.:
818-555-8372

E-mail Address:

▶ Put your markers on the START box. Pair A goes first.

▶ Pair A: Toss the coin. Move one or two boxes. Look at the picture in the box. If the picture has a check (✓), make an affirmative sentence. If the picture has an X, make a negative sentence.

Examples
Don't close the door.
Raise your hand.

▶ Pair B: Make sure the sentence is correct. If the sentence is *not* correct, Pair A's marker goes back to the box from their last turn.

▶ Pair B: Take your turn.

▶ If you land on the box where the other pair's marker is, move to the next box.

▶ If you land on the bottom of a ladder, go up to the top of the ladder and wait for your next turn. If you land on the top of a ladder, move to the next square.

▶ If you land on the top of a slide, go down to the bottom of the slide and wait for your next turn. If you land on the bottom of a slide, move to the next square.

▶ Continue to take turns. The first pair to get to the FINISH box wins.

▶ You each have some information, but the information is not complete. Cover your partner's side of the page.

▶ Student A: Look at your information. Ask Student B for the missing information in 1–4. Write the information.

▶ Student B: Look at your information. Ask Student A for the missing information in 5–8. Write the information.

Example:
A: Number 1. What day is April 20?
B: It's Tuesday.
A: Tuesday?
B: Right. Number 5. What time is it?
A: It's 3:50.
B: Could you repeat that?
A: 3:50.

▶ Take turns.

Student A's Information

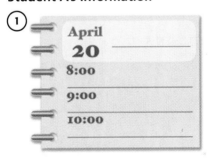 

Student B's Information

 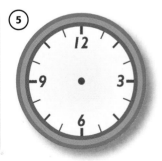

▶ Look at the ad for ten seconds.

▶ Ask and answer questions about the colors and prices.

▶ Take turns. Complete the list.

Example
A: What color are the pants?
B: Beige.
A: OK. And how much are they?
C: $29.99.
A: No. They're $19.99.
B: Right. They're $19.99. Next. What color is the _____?

Item	Price	Item	Price
beige pants	$29.99 $19.99		

▶ Student A, look at the picture of Kitchen A. Cover the picture of your partner's kitchen.

▶ Student B, look at the picture of Kitchen B. Cover the picture of your partner's kitchen.

▶ What's the same? What's different? Ask each other questions. Complete the chart.

Example
A: Is there a dishwasher?
B: Yes, there's a dishwasher.

	KITCHEN A	KITCHEN B
a dishwasher	There's no dishwasher.	There's a dishwasher.
a refrigerator		
a stove		
a microwave		
a table		
chairs		
a sink		
a window		
curtains		
blinds		
cabinets		

Unit 9: Slides and Ladders, PAGE 109

▶ Put your markers on the START box. Pair A goes first.

▶ Pair A: Toss the coin. Move one or two boxes. Look at the picture in the box and the words under the picture. Make a sentence.

Example
Mr. Chang doesn't want iced tea.

▶ Pair B: Make sure the sentence is correct. If the sentence is *not* correct, Pair A's marker goes back to the box from their last turn.

▶ Pair B: Take your turn.

▶ If you land on the box where the other pair's marker is, move to the next box.

▶ If you land on the bottom of a ladder, go up to the top of the ladder and wait for your next turn. If you land on the top of a ladder, move to the next square.

▶ If you land on the top of a slide, go down to the bottom of the slide and wait for your next turn. If you land on the bottom of a slide, move to the next square.

▶ Continue to take turns. The first pair to get to the FINISH box wins.

Unit 10: Does She Have a Fever?, PAGE 121

▶ Put your markers on the START box. Pair A goes first.

▶ Pair A: Toss the coin. Look at the picture in the box. Ask and answer a *yes / no* question with *have* or *feel*. The answer must be *No*!

Example
Student A: Does Tomas have a sore throat?
Student B: No he doesn't. He has a headache.

▶ Pair B: Make sure the conversation is correct. If the conversation is *not* correct, Pair A's marker goes back to the box from their last turn.

▶ Pair B: Take your turn.

▶ If you land on the box that has the other pair's marker, move to the next box.

▶ Continue to take turns. The first pair to get to the FINISH box wins.

Unit 11: Where? When? What Time? How Often?, PAGE 133

▶ Put your markers on the START box. Pair A goes first.

▶ Pair A: Toss the coin. Move one or two boxes. Student A, use the words below the picture to ask a question. Student B, give a true answer.

Example
How often / check e-mail?
Student A: How often do you check e-mail?
Student B: I check e-mail every day.

▶ Pair B: Make sure the conversation is correct. If the conversation is *not* correct, Pair A's marker goes back to the box from their last turn.

▶ Pair B: Take your turn.

▶ If you land on the box that has the other pair's marker, move to the next box.

▶ Continue to take turns. The first pair to get to the FINISH box wins.

Unit 12: City Planners Project, PAGE 145

▶ You are building a new city. Use the map.

▶ First, make a list of the buildings and places for your city. Then put the buildings on the map. Work together.

Example
Student A: Put the park on Market Street.
Student B: What about on California Avenue?
Student A: OK. Then put the apartment building here, next to the park.

Unit 13: Four in a Row, PAGE 157

▶ Try to get four boxes in a row, across →, down ↓, or diagonal ↘.

▶ Take turns. Student A goes first. Choose a box. Look at the picture and make a sentence. If there is an X in the box, make a negative sentence. Student B, make sure the sentence is correct.

▶ If the sentence is correct, write A (for Student A) or B (for Student B) in the box. You cannot choose a box with a letter already in it.

Example
Student A: Number 1. Igor is watching TV.
          OR
          Number 3. Cathy is not doing the laundry.
Student B: Right. (*Student A writes "A."*) My turn. Number _____.

▶ The first student to get four boxes in a row wins.

Unit 14: What's Happening?, PAGE 169

▶ Put your markers on the START box. Pair A goes first.

▶ Pair A: Toss the coin. Move one or two boxes. Read the word(s) in the box and look at the picture. Ask and answer a question.

Example
Student A: Who's crossing the street?
Student B: Bill is crossing the street.

▶ Pair B: Make sure the conversation is correct. If the conversation is *not* correct, Pair A's marker goes back to the box from their last turn.

▶ Pair B: Take your turn.

▶ If you land on the box that has the other pair's marker, move to the next box.

▶ Continue to take turns. The first pair to get to the FINISH box wins.

Unit 15: Can You . . . ?, PAGE 181

▶ Put your markers on the START box. Pair A goes first.

▶ Pair A: Toss the coin. Move one or two boxes. Look at the picture. Student A, ask a question. Student B, give a true answer. Answer with a short answer and add one sentence.

Example
Student A: Can you bake?
Student B: Yes, I can. I can bake cakes and pies.

▶ Pair B: Make sure the conversation is correct. If the conversation is *not* correct, Pair A's marker goes back to the box from their last turn.

▶ Pair B: Take your turn.

▶ If you land on the box that has the other pair's marker, move to the next box.

▶ Continue to take turns. The first pair to get to the FINISH box wins.

Unit 16: Where Were You?, PAGE 193

▶ Put your markers on the START box. Pair A goes first.

▶ Pair A: Toss the coin. Move one or two boxes.

▶ Student A, read the words in the box. Make a question.

▶ Student B, look at the information in the center of the game board and answer the question.

Example
Student A: Who was married on May 2?
Student B: Nina and Gerald.

▶ Pair B: Make sure the conversation is correct. If the conversation is *not* correct, Pair A's marker goes back to the box from their last turn.

▶ Pair B: Take your turn.

▶ If you land on the box that has the other pair's marker, move to the next box.

▶ Continue to take turns. The first pair to get to the FINISH box wins.

Audioscript

Unit 1: It's nice to meet you.

Listening, A and B, page 3

CONVERSATION 1

Tom:	Hi, I'm Tom Bailey.
Sharon:	Hi, I'm Sharon McLean.
Tom:	It's nice to meet you, Ms. McLean
Sharon:	It's nice to meet you, too. Please call me Sharon.
Tom:	And please call me Tom.

CONVERSATION 2

Norma:	Hello. I'm Norma Sanchez.
André:	Hi. My name is André Charles.
Norma:	It's nice to meet you, Mister Charles.
André:	It's nice to meet you, too. Please call me André.
Norma:	And please call me Norma.

Listening, A, page 7

Kim:	Hello. My name is Kim Rardin.
Rob:	Hi. I'm Rob Konrad.
Kim:	Nice to meet you, Rob.
Rob:	Nice to meet you, too. Excuse me. What's your last name again?
Kim:	It's Rardin—R-A-R-D-I-N. And your last name is . . . ?
Rob:	It's Konrad with a K. K-O-N-R-A-D.

Listening, B and C, page 7

CONVERSATION 1

Steve:	Who's that?
Rob:	Her name is Kim Rardin. She's nice.

CONVERSATION 2

Sylvia:	Who's that with Steve?
Kim:	His name is Rob Konrad. He's nice.

Grammar to Communicate 2, C, page 9

1. **A:** Who's that?
   B: That's my teacher. Her name is Ana. She's nice.
2. **A:** Who's that?
   B: That's my classmate. His name is Henry. He's nice.
3. **A:** Who's that?
   B: That's my friend. Her name is Barbara. She's nice.
4. **A:** Who's that man?
   B: His name is David.
   A: What's his last name?
   B: Hmm. I think his last name is Morton.

Unit 2: Are you from Mexico?

Listening, A and B, page 15

Jim:	Shanti, this is Bill. Bill, this is Shanti.
Shanti:	Nice to meet you, Bill.
Bill:	Nice to meet you, too.
Jim:	Shanti is from India.
Shanti:	Well, actually, I'm not from India. My parents are from India. I'm from England.
Jim:	You're from England? Sorry!
Shanti:	That's OK.

Listening, A and B, page 19

Bruce:	This is interesting! Some American foods aren't really American!
Denise:	Really?
Bruce:	Yes! Here. Try this. Is pizza American?
Denise:	No, it isn't. It's Italian.
Bruce:	You're right. OK. What about sandwiches? Are they American?
Denise:	Yes, they are!
Bruce:	Wrong! They're not American. They're British!
Denise:	Wow!

Grammar to Communicate 2, B, page 20

1. **A:** Are you Russian?
   B: Yes, I am. I'm from Moscow.
2. **A:** Is your teacher American?
   B: No, she isn't. She's Canadian.
3. **A:** Are Mr. and Mrs. Moon Korean?
   B: Yes, they are. They're from Seoul.
4. **A:** Is Léon French?
   B: No, he isn't. He's from Spain.
5. **A:** Are you and Masa Japanese?
   B: Yes, we are. We're from Tokyo.

Unit 3: Who's he?

Listening, A and B, page 27

Joe:	Is this a picture of your family?
Tania:	Yes, it is. But it's an old picture.
Joe:	Nice family. Who's this?
Tania:	He's my father. He's a doctor.
Joe:	An actor? Cool!
Tania:	No. Not an actor! A doctor!
Joe:	A doctor? Oh! And this is your mother, right?
Tania:	Uh-huh. She's an English teacher.
Joe:	Oh, that's great.

Grammar to Communicate 1, B, page 28

1. a salesperson
2. an artist
3. an assistant
4. a dentist
5. a lawyer
6. a homemaker
7. a painter
8. a bus driver
9. an engineer

Listening, A and B, page 31

Mrs. Silver: Is this a picture of your family?

Mrs. Santos: Yes. This is my son, Hector.

Mrs. Silver: How old is he?

Mrs. Santos: He's 18.

Mrs. Silver: He's cute.

Mrs. Santos: Thank you! And this is my daughter, Elena.

Mrs. Silver: She's cute, too. How old is she?

Mrs. Santos: She's 16. They're great kids.

Mrs. Silver: You're very lucky!

Unit 4: What's your phone number?

Listening, A and B, page 39

Greg: Hi, guys!

Sandra: Hi. So what's going on?

Ruth: Oh, our friends Ann and Mel are here from England.

Dario: Yeah, why don't you come over tonight?

Greg: OK. Call us later—on our cell phone.

Ruth: Good idea. What's your number?

Greg: It's 203-555-9342.

Ruth: 203-555-9342. OK.

Sandra: OK. See you later.

Dario: Great.

Grammar to Communicate 1, B, page 40

1. **A:** Hi. I'm Marie Dumonde. What are your names?
   B: Oscar and Agnes Leshek. Nice to meet you.
2. **A:** They're teachers. They're great.
   B: What are their names?
3. **A:** Mr. Davis, this is our daughter, Lana.
   B: Hi, Lana. Nice to meet you.
4. **A:** What's your address?
   B: Our address is 245 Baker Street.
   A: And what's your phone number?
   B: 202-555-5398.
5. **A:** Are these your children?
   B: Yes. Our daughter is 7. And our son is 4.

6. **A:** Come to the party tonight. It's at Ellen and Ron's house.
   B: Great! What's their address?
   A: 948 Elm Street.

Listening, A and B, page 43

CONVERSATION 1

Brad: Hi, Simone. It's Brad.

Simone: Hi, Brad. What's up?

Brad: Do you have Tom's cell phone number?

Simone: Sure. It's 310-555-3928.

Brad: 310-555-3928? OK. Thanks.

CONVERSATION 2

Brad: Hi, Tom. It's Brad. Where are you?

Tom: Hey, Brad. I'm at Alex's apartment. Come over!

Brad: OK. What's Alex's address?

Tom: It's 3674 Adams Street.

Brad: Could you repeat that, please?

Tom: 3674 Adams.

Brad: Thanks. See you soon.

Grammar to Communicate 2, B, page 44

1. **A:** Where is Tom?
   B: He's at Jack's house.
2. **A:** Where is Jun?
   B: He's at Mr. and Mrs. Park's apartment.
3. **A:** Where are Maggie and Ed?
   B: They're at Bob and Rita's house.
4. **A:** Where is Gabriela?
   B: She's at Lucy's office.
5. **A:** Where are Donna and Steve?
   B: They're at Mr. and Mrs. Randall's apartment.

Unit 5: Open your books.

Listening, A and B, page 51

Mike: OK, class, take out your workbooks. Wait. Where's my workbook?

Pierre: It's on your chair, Mike.

Mike: Oh, yeah. Thanks, Pierre. OK, so please open your workbooks to page 10. Astrid, please come to the board. Write sentence number 1.

Astrid: Excuse me, Mike, but where's the chalk?

Mike: The chalk? Hmm. Where's the chalk? Good question!

Javier: It's on your desk, Mike. It's over there, near the pens and pencils.

Mike: Oh, you're right, Javier. Thanks. Here's the chalk, Astrid.

Astrid: Thanks.

Mike: OK. Ready, Astrid? Wait! My glasses! Where are my glasses?

Astrid: In your hand! They're in your hand, Mike.

Grammar to Communicate 1, D, page 53

1. **A:** Where are the books?
   B: They're in the closet.
2. **A:** Where are the dictionaries?
   B: They're in the bookcase.
3. **A:** Where is the pencil?
   B: It's on the desk.
4. **A:** Where are the books?
   B: They're in the backpack.
5. **A:** Where are the notebooks?
   B: They're on the chairs.

Listening, A and B, page 55

Mike: Julio, please close the door. Thanks. OK, everyone. Are you ready for the test? Remember. Write your answers on the answer sheet. Don't write on the test. Use a pencil. Don't use a pen. Listen to the CD. Is everyone ready? OK. Listen carefully.

Unit 6: It's Monday morning.

Listening, A and B, page 63

WEATHER REPORT 1

And now for today's weather. It's Monday, so—of course—it's rainy. Yes, it's another rainy Monday. And it's only 53 degrees, so it's cool. Take your umbrellas and your raincoats.

WEATHER REPORT 2

Good morning, everybody! Today is Wednesday, and here's today's weather. It's cloudy and it's already 85 degrees out! Yes, it's another hot day in New York.

WEATHER REPORT 3

Hello, everyone. It's Thursday, and here's today's weather. It's a beautiful, warm day. It's just a little windy. The temperature is now 72 degrees. It's a perfect day!

Grammar to Communicate 1, B, page 64

1. **A:** What day is today?
   B: It's Monday.
2. **A:** What's the weather today?
   B: It's cloudy.
3. **A:** What's the temperature?
   B: It's 85 degrees.
4. **A:** What day is today?
   B: It's Friday.

5. **A:** What's the weather today?
   B: It's sunny.
6. **A:** What's the temperature?
   B: It's 60 degrees.

Listening, A and B, page 67

CONVERSATION 1

Frank: What time is it?
Ted: It's 8:40.
Frank: Oh, wow! I'm late. My English class is at 8:45.

CONVERSATION 2

John: Where do you work, Bill?
Bill: At the bookstore.
John: What are your work hours?
Bill: 3 to 7, Monday and Thursday.

CONVERSATION 3

Elena: When is your test?
Tina: On Friday.
Elena: What time?
Tina: At 10 in the morning.

Unit 7: These jeans are on sale.

Listening, A and B, page 75

Marcy: OK. What's on my list? A polo shirt for Joe.
Lois: Here they are.
Marcy: Oh, yeah? Great!
Lois: How about this shirt?
Marcy: Perfect. What else is on my list? A sweater—for me! Where are the sweaters?
Lois: Over here. Look. These sweaters are on sale today, too. Buy one, get one free.
Marcy: Oh! That sweater is cute. And here's my size.
Lois: Hey, here's an idea. How about *you* buy one, and *I* get one free?

Grammar to Communicate 1, D, page 77

1. Is this blouse on sale?
2. Those socks are my favorite kind.
3. That jacket is nice.
4. Are these jeans on sale?
5. This T-shirt is a great color.
6. These shirts are cool.

Listening, A and B, page 79

Daughter: Dad! It's Mom's birthday next week. Let's go to the K. Hill Web site for her gift.
Father: Great idea. OK. What about a blouse for her new skirt?
Daughter: OK. Look. These blouses are really pretty. And they're on sale.

Father:	Good. How much are they?
Daughter:	They're $29.99. The regular price is $39.99.
Father:	Great. She's a size medium.
Daughter:	What color is her new skirt?
Father:	Color? I don't know. Black . . . or blue . . . or brown?
Daughter:	I know! Let's get a white blouse!
Father:	Perfect!

Grammar to Communicate 2, C, page 80

1. The pants are $18.99.
2. The dress is $24.99.
3. The shoes are $17.99.
4. The socks are $2.99.
5. The T-shirt is $5.99.
6. The coat is $79.99.
7. The shirts are $24.99.
8. The blouse is $15.99.

Unit 8: There's a sunny kitchen.

Listening, A and B, page 87

Mrs. Garcia:	Honey, listen. Here's a nice apartment.
Mr. Garcia:	Oh, yeah? What's it like?
Mrs. Garcia:	Well, there's a modern kitchen.
Mr. Garcia:	Good.
Mrs. Garcia:	And there's a small dining room, a sunny living room, and two bathrooms.
Mr. Garcia:	Uh-huh. How many bedrooms?
Mrs. Garcia:	That's the best part. There are three bedrooms. And there are a lot of closets.
Mr. Garcia:	You're right. It's great.
Mrs. Garcia:	But it's not perfect. There's carpeting, but there are no blinds.

Grammar to Communicate 1, D, page 89

Realtor:	This apartment is great.
Customer:	Really? What's it like?
Realtor:	There's a sunny kitchen.
Customer:	That's good.
Realtor:	And there's a nice living room.
Customer:	Uh-huh.
Realtor:	There are two bedrooms. One bedroom is big and one bedroom is small.
Customer:	That's OK. What about a dining room?
Realtor:	There's no dining room. The kitchen is an eat-in kitchen.
Customer:	Oh. What about closets?
Realtor:	There's a closet in the big bedroom, and there are two closets in the hall.

Customer:	Oh, good. And the bathroom?
Realtor:	There's a big bathroom.

Listening, A and B, page 91

Realtor:	There's a great three-bedroom apartment for rent on Adams Street.
Mrs. Garcia:	Really? What's the kitchen like?
Realtor:	Oh, it's big. There's a window over the sink, so it's nice and sunny.
Mrs. Garcia:	Wonderful! Is there a dishwasher?
Realtor:	Yes, there is. And there's a microwave.
Mrs. Garcia:	That's good. Are there any blinds on the window?
Realtor:	No, there aren't. There are curtains.

Unit 9: I want a turkey sandwich.

Listening, A and B, page 99

CONVERSATION PART 1

Waiter:	Are you ready to order?
Mom:	Yes, we are. Just sandwiches today, please. I want a grilled chicken sandwich. And my son wants a tuna salad sandwich.
Waiter:	Very good.

CONVERSATION PART 2, LATER

Waiter:	Anything for dessert?
Mom:	Yes! For dessert, my son wants chocolate cake.
Joey:	I like chocolate!
Waiter:	Excellent!
Mom:	Oh, and we both need forks.
Waiter:	Certainly. That's one chocolate cake and two forks.

Listening, A and B, page 103

CONVERSATION PART 1

Waiter:	Here you are, ma'am. Here's the salt.
Mrs. Brock:	I don't need salt. I need sugar!
Waiter:	Oh, sorry.

CONVERSATION PART 2, A FEW MINUTES LATER

Mr. Brock:	Excuse me, waiter?
Waiter:	Yes, sir?
Mr. Brock:	My wife doesn't like her soup. It's cold.
Waiter:	Oh, sorry.

CONVERSATION PART 3, A FEW MINUTES LATER

Waiter:	More coffee, folks?
Mrs. Brock:	We don't want more coffee. We want more iced tea.
Waiter:	Oh, sorry.

Unit 10: Do you have a fever?

Listing, A and B, page 111

CONVERSATION 1

Doctor:	Hello, Ms. Curtis. Hi, Ray. How are you today?
Ray:	I'm sick. I have a sore throat.
Doctor:	OK. Let's see. Open your mouth and say "Ah."
Ray:	Ah.
Doctor:	Hmm.
Mother:	What is it, Doctor Baum?
Doctor:	He's right. His throat is very red.

CONVERSATION 2

Doctor:	Hello, Mrs. Silver. Hi, Max.
Max:	Hello, Doctor Baum.
Doctor:	What's the matter?
Mother:	He has an earache.
Doctor:	OK. Let's look. This ear?
Max:	No. This ear.

Grammar to Communicate 1, C, page 112

1. **Doctor:** What's the matter?
   Patient: I have the flu.
2. **Doctor:** How is Andy today?
   Mother: He has an earache.
3. **Doctor:** What's the matter?
   Patient: I have a cough.
4. **Doctor:** How are May and Jen today?
   Father: They have sore throats.

Listing, A and B, page 115

Eli:	Hi, Gail. Are you OK?
Gail:	No. I feel sick.
Eli:	Oh. Why? What's wrong?
Gail:	I have the flu.
Eli:	Oh, no! Do you have a fever?
Gail:	Yes, I do. I feel very hot.
Eli:	Go home!

Grammar to Communicate 2, D, page 117

1. **A:** Does Emily have a headache?
   B: Yes, she does.
2. **A:** Do Dmitri and Natasha feel tired?
   B: Yes, they do.
3. **A:** Does Khalil want tea?
   B: Yes, he does.
4. **A:** Do Mr. and Mrs. Ahn feel nauseous?
   B: No, they don't.

Unit 11: I always do the dishes.

Listing, A and B, page 123

Mom:	How is everything, honey?
Cara:	Fine, Mom. I'm just tired.
Mom:	You work hard!
Cara:	I know. Allan works hard, too.
Mom:	Of course. Does he ever help you at home?
Cara:	Sure! He sometimes cooks dinner. We take turns.
Mom:	Good. What about the dishes?
Cara:	Well, uh, no, he never does the dishes.
Mom:	Really?
Cara:	Yes, I always do the dishes, and Allan checks e-mail.
Mom:	I see.

Listing, A and B, page 127

CONVERSATION 1

Reporter:	Hello. May I ask your name?
Natasha:	Sure. It's Natasha.
Reporter:	Hi, Natasha. So, what do you do for fun on the weekend?
Natasha:	Oh, my friends and I go dancing.
Reporter:	Great. How often do you go?
Natasha:	Every weekend! We usually go on Friday nights.
Reporter:	Really? And what time do you go?
Natasha:	Around 11:00.

CONVERSATION 2

Reporter:	Hello. And your name is . . . ?
Colin:	Colin.
Reporter:	So, Colin, what do you do for fun on the weekend?
Colin:	Oh, my girlfriend and I usually go to the movies.
Reporter:	Great. When do you go?
Colin:	We usually go on Saturday night.
Reporter:	That's a popular movie night! Where do you go?
Colin:	To Cinema 24, mostly. It's crowded, but it's fun.

Unit 12: It's next to the bank.

Listing, A and B, page 135

Abdir:	Do you like your new neighborhood?
Noel:	Yes, I do. It's very convenient. There are a lot of stores near my apartment building.

Abdir: Oh, really?

Noel: Uh-huh. And there's a bank right around the corner, on Park Avenue.

Abdir: That's great.

Noel: Yeah, and next to the bank, there's a coffee shop.

Abdir: Oh, yeah?

Noel: Yeah. And there's a post office across the street from my building.

Abdir: Terrific! Where's your apartment, again?

Noel: It's on the corner of Jefferson Street and Garden Avenue.

Grammar to Communicate 1, D, page 137

1. **A:** Excuse me. Is there a park near here?
   B: Yes. There's a park on Adams Street. It's next to the restaurant.

2. **A:** Excuse me. Is there a library near here?
   B: Yes. There's a library on the corner of Water Street and Adams Street.

3. **A:** Excuse me. Is there a restaurant near here?
   B: Yes. There's a restaurant on the corner of Adams Street and Baker Street.

4. **A:** Excuse me. Is there a bank near here?
   B: Yes. There's a bank on Water Street. It's next to the department store.

5. **A:** Excuse me. Is there a hospital near here?
   B: Yes. There's a hospital on the corner of Adams Street and Water Street.

Listening, A and B, page 139

Interviewer: Excuse me, ma'am. Can I ask you a question or two?

Shopper: OK.

Interviewer: Do you usually get all your groceries at the supermarket?

Shopper: Yes. Everyone in my family has favorite foods and the supermarket has everything.

Interviewer: Everything?

Shopper: Yes. For example, my daughter likes chocolate chip cookies and I buy them there.

Interviewer: I see.

Shopper: And my son likes a special kind of soap and the supermarket always has it.

Interviewer: So you shop at the supermarket because it has everything?

Shopper: Yes. Oh, and the prices are good. That's very important.

Grammar to Communicate 2, C, page 140

1. **A:** Marie likes chocolate cake.
   B: I know. She has it every day for dessert.

2. **A:** How often do you eat eggs?
   B: We have them two times a week.

3. **A:** Do you eat breakfast every day?
   B: Yes, but sometimes I have it at work.

4. **A:** Do you need those spoons?
   B: No, you can use them.

5. **A:** Do your kids like fish?
   B: No, they never eat it.

6. **A:** Do you want hamburgers tonight?
   B: OK. Let's have them with French fries.

Unit 13: I'm talking on the phone.

Listening, A and B, page 147

CONVERSATION 1

Son: Dad, are you busy?

Father: Not really. I'm reading the newspaper.

Son: Oh, yeah. You read the newspaper every night.

Father: That's right. So, what's up?

Son: I'm studying for a test. Can you help me?

Father: Of course! What's the subject?

Son: English.

Father: Uh, where's your mother?

CONVERSATION 2

Mom: Where's your sister Emma? It's 6:30—time for dinner.

Son: I bet she's talking on her cell phone.

Mom: You're probably right. She and her friends talk on the phone all the time. Look in her room.

Son: No, she isn't there, Mom.

Mom: Is she in the living room?

Son: Yup. She's sleeping on the sofa!

Grammar to Communicate 1, B, page 148

1. **A:** Where is Kevin?
   B: He's in his bedroom. He's studying.

2. **A:** Where are Helena and Sara?
   B: They're in their room. They're checking e-mail.

3. **A:** Where are you?
   B: I'm in the living room. I'm listening to music.

4. **A:** Where are Dan and Maggie?
   B: They're in the bedroom. They're playing video games.

5. **A:** Where is Andrea?
   B: She's sleeping. Be quiet!

6. **A:** Where are you and Marie?
   B: We're in the kitchen. We're helping Rose with her homework.

Listening, A and B, page 151

Luis: Hi, Mrs. Soto. Is Eric home?

Mrs. Soto: Yes, he is. He's making his bed. He makes his bed every morning. Eric? Luis is here. What are you doing?

Eric: Wait, Mom. Don't come in.

Mrs. Soto: Eric! You aren't making your bed! You're playing video games!

Eric: I'm not playing video games, Mom. I'm checking e-mail.

Unit 14: Are you walking to school?

Listening, A and B, page 159

CONVERSATION 1

A: Hi. Where are you?

B: I'm on my way to school.

A: Are you taking the bus?

B: No, I'm not. I'm riding my bike.

A: Well, don't talk on the phone! Be careful!

CONVERSATION 2

A: Hi. Where are you?

B: We're in the car.

A: Is Henry driving?

B: Yes, he is.

A: Are you wearing your seat belt?

B: Of course!

CONVERSATION 3

A: Hi. Where are you?

B: We're on our way to school.

A: Are you taking the subway?

B: No, we're not. We're taking the bus.

A: Oh, OK.

Listening, A and B, page 163

CONVERSATION PART 1

Officer 1: Who's driving the car?

Officer 2: The driver is a man. He's about 20 years old.

Officer 1: Look! He's going straight on Mill Avenue.

Officer 2: What's he doing now?

Officer 1: He's turning left on Adams Street.

Officer 2: No, wait. Now he's turning right on Richmond Street.

Officer 1: Where is he going now?

Officer 2: He's going straight on Richmond Street.

CONVERSATION PART 2

Officer 2: Now he's stopping. Why is he stopping?

Officer 1: He's parking the car. Let's go!

Officer 2: Get out of the car! Hands up!

Young man: What's the problem, officer?

Officer 1: You're driving a stolen car.

Young man: No, I'm not! This is my mother's car!

Grammar to Communicate 2, C, page 165

1. **A:** Where are you going?
   B: We're going to work.
2. **A:** Who's driving?
   B: My father is driving.
3. **A:** What's he driving?
   B: He's driving a dark blue car.
4. **A:** Where is she getting off?
   B: She's getting off near her house.
5. **A:** Who are they going with?
   B: They're going with their parents.
6. **A:** What's she doing?
   B: She's walking to work.

Unit 15: My boyfriend can't sing.

Listening, A and B, page 171

Kate: What's your boyfriend like?

Jane: He's very funny. He can tell jokes and funny stories.

Kate: Oh, really?

Jane: Yes, and he's talented, too.

Kate: Oh, yeah?

Jane: Yeah. He can play the guitar and sing.

Kate: Wow! Is he a good cook, too?

Jane: Oh, no. He can't cook. And he can't fix things. He's not good with machines.

Kate: That's OK. Does he have a brother?

Grammar to Communicate 1, D, page 173

Antonio: What's your girlfriend like?

Hector: She's a great artist. She can draw and she can paint. Here are some of her pictures.

Antonio: Wow! They're beautiful.

Hector: Thanks. She's a great cook, too.

Antonio: Oh, yeah?

Hector: Yeah. She can cook Italian food! And she can bake. She makes delicious chocolate cake.

Antonio: Wow! So, is she a good singer, too?

Hector: Oh, no. She can't sing. And she can't dance.

Antonio: Too bad. You're a good dancer.

Listening, A and B, page 175

Helen: I need a job. Do you have any ideas?

Eddie: What can you do?

Helen: Well, I can take care of children.

Eddie: Can you work during the day?

Helen: Yes, I can. I go to school in the evenings.

Eddie:	Then maybe you can work in a day-care center.
Helen:	Good idea! But do I need a degree?
Eddie:	I don't know. Good question! Ask the job counselor at your school.

Grammar to Communicate 2, C, page 176

1. **A:** Can you use office machines?
   B: Yes, I can. I use a computer and a copier at work.
2. **A:** Can Ms. DaSilva fix cars?
   B: No, she can't. She's not good with cars.
3. **A:** Can Mr. Yeoh work weekends?
   B: Yes, he can. He has another job during the week.
4. **A:** Can Fran take care of animals?
   B: No, she can't. She doesn't like them.
5. **A:** Can you and Fred use computers?
   B: Yes, we can. We work in a bank.

Unit 16: We were at home.

Listening, A and B, page 183

Pierre:	Hi, Charlotte. Where were you last week? You weren't at work.
Charlotte:	No, I was in Miami.
Pierre:	Oh, yeah?
Charlotte:	Yeah. I was at my cousin Gina's wedding last Saturday.
Pierre:	How was the wedding?
Charlotte:	Beautiful. The weather was great. Everyone was so happy.
Pierre:	What about the party?
Charlotte:	Oh, it was a lot of fun. About 50 people were there—family, friends, co-workers.
Pierre:	*I* wasn't there.
Charlotte:	Of course you weren't there. You don't know Gina!

Listening, A and B, page 187

CONVERSATION PART 1

Ramon:	Where were you last week?
Liz:	I was on vacation—at Disney World.
Ramon:	Disney World? I love Disney World. It's fantastic!
Liz:	I know! When were *you* there?
Ramon:	Last year. At the end of June. We were there for ten days.
Liz:	Were you there on July 4?
Ramon:	Yes! The fireworks were great!

CONVERSATION PART 2

| Liz: | Who were you there with? You don't have kids. |

Ramon:	No. I was there with my wife. Just the two of us.
Liz:	Really?
Ramon:	Yeah. Why are you so surprised?
Liz:	I don't know. People usually go there with their kids.
Ramon:	Well, actually, we were on our honeymoon! It was very romantic.
Liz:	Oh!
Ramon:	Yup! We were married last June 24.

Grammar to Communicate 2, C, page 189

1. **A:** Where were you on New Year's Eve?
   B: I was at a restaurant in the city.
   A: Who were you there with?
   B: My wife and some friends.
2. **A:** When were you on vacation?
   B: In June. We were in San Diego.
   A: How was the weather?
   B: It was great. It was sunny and warm.

Pronunciation Activities

Unit 1, A, 3, page 197

a. It's nice to meet you, too.
b. I'm Pat Logan.
c. My name is Robin North.

B, 2 and 3, page 197

a. He's my classmate.
b. She's nice.
c. She's the teacher.
d. He's cute.
e. He's my friend.

Unit 3, A, 3, page 199

a. a homemaker
b. an artist
c. an engineer
d. a painter
e. a doctor

B, 2 and 3, page 199

a. Where are your children?
b. They are in Dallas, with my parents.
c. How old are they?
d. My son is ten.
e. My daughter is seven.
f. They are great kids.

Unit 4, A, 2 and 3, page 200

a. Our teacher is great.

b. Your son is cute.

c. What's their phone number?

d. What's your address?

e. Their children are in high school.

f. Here's our e-mail address.

Unit 5, B, 2 and 3, page 201

a. Please erase the board.

b. Turn to page 23.

c. Copy the words in your notebooks.

d. Take out a pencil and an eraser.

Unit 6, A, 2 and 3, page 202

a. degrees

b. again

c. listen

d. favorite

e. temperature

Unit 7, A, 2 and 3, page 203

a. that blouse

b. those sneakers

c. this shirt

d. these pants

e. these socks

f. those jeans

g. that T-shirt

h. this suit

B, 3, page 203

a. twelve eighty-five

b. forty-seven dollars

c. sixty-three ninety-seven

d. ten seventy-five

e. a dollar eighty-nine

f. two twenty-five

Unit 8, A, 3, page 204

a. There's carpeting in the bedroom.

b. There's no dining room.

c. There are blinds on the windows.

d. There's a big kitchen.

e. There are two bathrooms.

Unit 9, A, 2 and 3, page 205

a. Ms. Rios likes chocolate cake, but her husband likes apple pie.

b. Nabil wants a grilled cheese sandwich, but Dan wants a grilled chicken sandwich.

c. My son likes pizza, but my daughter likes spaghetti.

B, 3, page 205

a. The baby doesn't want juice now.

b. We don't like soda.

c. Mr. and Mrs. Song don't need milk for their coffee.

d. Will doesn't want dessert.

e. The soup doesn't need salt.

f. Eleni doesn't like chocolate.

Unit 10, A, 3, page 206

a. My daughter has a fever.

b. We have the flu.

c. Ms. Sayed has a cough.

d. Misha has a backache.

e. I have a cold.

f. Mr. Ito has a stomachache

B, 2 and 3, page 206

a. Do they have aspirin?

b. Do we need cough medicine?

c. Do you want water?

d. Do they feel better now?

e. Do you have a sore throat?

f. Do we want chicken soup?

Unit 11, B, 2 and 3, page 207

a. How often does he visit you?

b. What time does she play soccer?

c. When does he relax?

d. Where does she eat out?

e. How often does she get a DVD?

f. When does he watch TV?

Unit 12, B, 3, page 208

a. My kids like cookies. I buy them every week.

b. Can you get milk? We need it for our coffee.

c. We eat a lot of ice cream. We have it for dessert.

d. Eggs are sometimes expensive. I buy them on sale.

e. Do you like salad? I eat it every day.

Unit 13, A, 2 and 3, page 209

a. They're checking e-mail.

b. What do you do in your free time?

c. He's talking on his cell phone.

d. She's helping in the kitchen.

e. We're watching TV in the living room.

B, 3, page 209

a. Mr. Soto isn't getting the mail.

b. Kyung isn't taking out the trash.

c. Noemi and Keiko aren't checking e-mail.

d. My mother and I aren't doing the laundry.

e. Bernie isn't fixing the window.

f. You aren't helping!

Unit 14, A, 3, page 210

a. Is Monica taking the subway?
Yes, she is.

b. Is Jerry riding his bike?
No, he isn't.

c. Are your parents taking a taxi?
Yes, they are.

d. Are you on your way home?
No, we aren't.

e. Are you driving now?
Yes, I am.

B, 2 and 3, page 210

a. What are they doing?

b. Who are we waiting for?

c. Where are you turning?

d. When are they going to work?

e. Who are you talking to?

f. Where are you parking?

Unit 15, A, 2 and 3, page 211

a. Joe can play the piano.

b. I can't sew.

c. His children can't cook.

d. Rick can tell jokes.

e. My mother can knit.

f. Sue can't bake cakes.

B, 3, page 211

a. Can you paint?
Yes, I can.

b. Can he cook?
No, he can't.

c. Can they draw?
Yes, they can.

d. Can she play the guitar?
Yes, she can.

e. Can you dance?
No, I can't.

Unit 16, A, 2 and 3, page 212

a. Dalia wasn't in school last night.

b. Ling and I were at the mall yesterday.

c. Mr. and Mrs. Oh were in the park on Sunday.

d. Tomiko wasn't at home last Friday night.

e. They weren't at the beach on Saturday.

f. The wedding was beautiful.

B, 2 and 3, page 212

a. Was he at work yesterday?

b. Was she there in March?

c. Was he in Lima last year?

d. Was she in the U.S. in 2006?

e. Was she on vacation last week?

f. Was he with you in Orlando?

Index

ACADEMIC SKILLS

Grammar

a / an, 28

adjectives

    demonstrative, 76

    possessive, 4, 9, 40, 48

adverbs of frequency, 124

affirmative statements, 16, 100, 148, 172, 180

be, 4, 16, 20, 32, 64, 68, 168, 184, 188, 192

can, 172, 176

cannot, 172

consonants and vowels, 28

contractions, 4, 5, 8, 16, 20, 32, 44, 56, 64, 72, 88, 104,
    148, 164, 172, 184

have, 112, 113, 116, 117, 120

have, feel, need, want, 116, 117

imperatives, 56, 57

information questions, 32–34, 64, 68, 69, 128, 129, 164,
    165, 177, 180

it / them, 140, 141

negative statements, 16, 104, 152, 172, 180

nouns

    plural, 52, 60

    possessive, 44, 45, 48

    singular, 28

on / in, 53

prepositions of location, 136, 137

pronouns

    object, 140, 141

    subject, 8, 12, 16, 20, 40

there is / there are, 88, 92, 96

this / that / these / those, 76, 77

verb tense

    present progressive, 148, 152, 156, 160, 164

    simple past, 184, 188, 189, 192

    simple present, 100, 104, 112, 116, 117, 120, 128

verbs

    irregular, 112, 124

want / like / need, 100, 104, 108

yes / no questions, 20, 21, 24, 92, 96, 116, 117, 120, 160,
    161, 168, 176, 180, 188, 192

Listening

addresses, 39, 43

apartments, 87, 90, 91

clothing, 74, 79

conversations, 2, 3, 5, 7, 9, 15, 19, 20, 27, 31, 39, 40, 43,
    44, 51, 53, 62, 64, 67, 75, 79, 87, 89, 91, 99, 103,
    111, 112, 115, 117, 123, 127, 135, 137, 139, 140,
    147, 148, 151, 159, 160, 163, 165, 171, 173, 175,
    176, 183, 187

countries and nationalities, 15

families, 27

food and drink, 19, 102, 103

health, 111, 115, 117

instructions, 55

introductions, 2, 3, 15

job duties, 175

letters of alphabet, 6

locations, 51

neighborhoods, 135

numbers, 38, 42, 43

occupations, 27, 28

schedules, 66, 67

shopping, 75, 79, 139

talents and abilities, 171, 175

time, 67

transportation, 159, 163

vacations, 187

weather, 62, 63

weddings, 183

Reading

abbreviations, 94, 118

activities and routines, 123, 150

addresses, 40

ads, 94, 178

calendars, 186

catalogs, 82

daily planners, 69, 182

dates, 182, 186

eating problem, 106

e-mails, 70, 142, 154, 166

family members, 34

food, 22

graphs, 130

holidays, 190

instructions, 55, 56

job duties, 175

letters, 34, 106

maps, 14, 42, 136, 137, 144, 145, 163

menus, 101

names, 40

neighborhoods, 135, 136

numbers, 30, 42, 186

occupations, 34

patient information forms, 118, 119

personal information forms, 10, 49

schedules, 66

test applications, 58

time, 66

transportation, 162, 165

Speaking

Writing

LIFESKILLS

Business and Employment

Consumer Education

Environment and World

Government and Community

Health and Nutrition

Interpersonal Communication

People